ADAM SCHALL
A Jesuit at the Court of China

In this century China has been able to congratulate herself on the possession of two men remarkable for their science and their virtue: Father Matthew Ricci and this, our master — Father John Adam Schall.

The Minister of Finance in Peking, October 9, 1623.

If one wishes to get to know the way by which a man approaches God, it is necessary to enter into his particular point of departure. A fortiori *is that necessary if one has the task of helping him to travel along the road. And that is the ABC of every apostolate.*

Dom Pierre-Célestin Lou Tseng-Tsiang: Ways of Confucius
and of Christ (London, 1948).

John Adam Schall, (1592-1666), from a portrait published
the year after his death.

ADAM SCHALL

A Jesuit at the Court of China

1592 - 1666

RACHEL ATTWATER
adapted from the French of Joseph Duhr, S.J.

THE BRUCE PUBLISHING COMPANY
MILWAUKEE

Much of the material in this book was first published in *Un Jésuite en Chine, Adam Schall,* by Joseph Duhr, S.J., by Desclée de Brouwer, Paris, in 1936.

Nihil obstat: Josephus Cartmell, S.T.D. Censor deputatus
Imprimatur: Dionysius McDonnell, Vic.Gen.
Liverpolii, die 18a februarii, 1963

Contents

Acknowledgements

The portrait of John Adam Schall used in the frontispiece is from *China*, by Fr. A. Kircher, published in 1667, one year after Schall's death.

Plates I and II are taken from *Fonti Ricciane*, Vol II, *Storia dell'Introduzione del Cristianesimo in Cina*, (Roma, La Libreria dello Stato, 1949). Plates III and IV are taken from *A Description of the Empire of China and Chinese Tartary, from the French of Père J. B. du Halde, Jesuit*, Vol II, (London, 1741).

The publishers wish to acknowledge the courtesy of the Jesuit Fathers of Farm Street, London, for the use of their library and their help in obtaining these illustrations.

List of Illustrations

Introduction

THIS is an admirable book, well planned and beautifully executed. It can confidently be assumed that any reader who allows himself to be caught up in the story will not be able to put it down until he has devoured that last word. The story reads like a fairytale, indeed has something miraculous about it, but is true and historical in almost every detail, as Rachel Attwater so well shows. John Adam Schall came of a prosperous and noble Cologne family, and had the world at his feet. But when hardly out of his boyhood, he renounced all his bright prospects to become a Jesuit in Rome. There he had come into contact with Father Nicholas Trigault, a missionary from China who had known the great pioneer Matteo Ricci and was in Europe to obtain men and funds to carry on his heroic, patient enterprise. Schall was one of the many he set on fire. John Adam, still very young, wrote to petition the Jesuit General that he might be assigned to the Chinese mission after the completion of his studies and his ordination, which took place in 1618, when he was twenty-six. His petition had been granted and from that moment his beloved humanistic studies were abandoned for the harder grind of mathematics and science, which he knew to be essential for his future mission. Inspired by the example of the expiatory toil of his patron Adam, the father of us all to whom he was tenderly devoted, the merry fun-loving Rhinelander applied himself with so much intensity and perseverance to his new tasks that he became eventually a master mathematician and an astronomer of high quality. At the very time, 1618, when he set sail from Lisbon for his land of heart's desire, a Jesuit in China had translated Galileo's epoc-making *Starry Messenger,* with its implied Copernicanism, into Chinese and, though Copernicanism had no future for a long time in the West owing to the unfortunate and misguided action of Pope Urban VIII in condemning Galileo, it became the accepted doctrine of the Jesuits and their pupils in China and Japan.

After a nightmare voyage of disease, starvation and mutiny, Schall's ship eventually reached Goa, sadly depleted of missionaries. He did not get to the Portuguese settlement of Macao, that little doorway to China with its amazing powers of survival, until July 1619, and then only to find that the Christians of China were undergoing one of their periodic experiences of severe persecution. Among the six expelled Jesuits there was a Father Vagnoni who had preached Christ our Lord a little too openly in Nanking and had been bastinadoed for his pains. A companion missionary expelled with him in a narrow wooden cage with chains round neck and feet in which they were confined for a month, recorded that Father Vagnoni's feet took a month to recover from the bastinado. It was this man who introduced Father Schall to the mysteries of the Chinese language and also, in a fashion he did not himself fully realize, to the mystery of the Chinese mind, which refuses to be hurried in the way he had tried to hurry it. Father Schall was one quick to learn. In 1622, after he had been three years sweating at the Chinese language and finding out all he could about the Chinese mind, he suddenly found himself in a new role. The Calvinist Dutch made an assault on Macao which would have been fatal to all Christian prospects in the Far East if successful. Schall who came of a warrior race seized a musket and tackled the foe, as did the other Jesuits, the friars, and the Portuguese in general. The attack was so vigorous and unexpected that the Dutch fled to their ships in terror. In the mêlée Schall captured a Dutch captain but what he did with him is not recorded.

Schall quickly realized that a western man as such would never be accepted by the Chinese. To preach Christ to the Chinese the man of the West must himself become a Chinese, as Matteo Ricci had done. Years earlier, John Adam had relinquished brilliant worldly prospects, relatives, fatherland and familiar ways. Now he must go a step further by adopting Chinese dress and a Chinese name. He put on the silk robes and headgear of a Chinese scholar and took to himself the name of T'ang Jo-wang. As the persecution had subsided owing to the death of its chief fomentor, Schall in his new guise was given permission to enter China and to proceed to Peking. To make a long story short, this was the beginning of an apostolic career as full of perils, persecutions, matchless courage, patience, failures, unbelievable triumph, and finally a living martyrdom, as any in the long history of the Church. Even some of his own superiors had doubts about Adam Schall. He was too genial, too buoyant, too outspoken for their conservative tastes. But he won them over, as he did the jealous Chinese astronomers, by his invincible good temper, his well known kindness to all in trouble, his unflagging devotion to his priestly duties, which always came first in his consideration. Once, a Christian army general had fallen into the hands of his enemies and been condemned to death. Two days before his execution, a seller of coal with blackened face and a sack on his back entered the prison. It was Adam Schall, come to bring the comfort of the sacraments to the condemned man and another Christian also under sentence. He managed to stay with them right up to the time of their execution and by his own high courage and shining faith sent them to Heaven with great cheerfulness and serenity. Under a new Chinese dynasty, Schall was promoted a mandarin of the first class and made director of the Chinese

Institute of Astronomy. He tried hard to escape the unwanted honours but the Emperor who admired him wholeheartedly insisted, and he became, in fact, the second most important man in the entire Chinese Empire. He had the run of the Forbidden City itself where the Emperor lived, a most extraordinary concession. Never in his high position did he omit to say his daily Mass, and no matter how busy he might be he excused himself from no part of the Divine Office. He instructed and baptized close on three hundred Christians each year, in spite of his overwhelming duties at court and the Institute of Astronomy. He had truly the faith that moves mountains. Towards the end of his life when he had become paralysed, a powerful enemy succeded in having him cast into chains and condemned to death before three successive courts, first by strangulation, then by beheading and finally by the most barbarous of all deaths known to Chinese law. His whole heroic life proved his willingness, his eagerness, to die like and for his Divine Master. But the heavens came to the aid of the man who had plotted their courses with such loving care, first a comet, then an earthquake, and finally a devouring fire.

This brief introduction has touched only on a few points in a splendidly told story. John Adam Schall was assuredly one of the greatest men in the history of the Society of Jesus, which has produced its fair quota of such people. He had his faults which his most competent biographer very honestly discusses. At the last he made a most moving public confession of them which she reproduces. His successor at the Institute of Astronomy in better times, the lovable and brave Belgian Ferdinand Verbiest, who had himself been condemned to death, was with him to the last, to speak for the paralyzed hero who could no longer speak.

It would be impossible to speak of this book in too laudatory terms. Let the reader try it and see for himself.

James Brodrick, S.J.

The Son of Heaven
and the Celestial Doctrine

I N the autumn of the year of our Lord 1630 a Jesuit priest, John Adam Schall, arrived in Peking. This was not his first visit to that great city of the Chinese Empire; he had spent some time there a few years previously before being put in charge of the Christian mission at the town of Sianfu. Since he had left his home in Cologne twenty-two years ago, at the age of just sixteen, he seemed to have spent much of his life waiting for this moment, preparing for this mission which was to exercise all his talents, all his resources of personality and of faith. Now at last the long years of preparation for priesthood in Rome, of delay at Goa on the journey East and at the Portuguese colony of Macao waiting for a favourable time to enter into the enclosed and to some extent hostile Chinese Empire, were over. The field of his dedicated apostleship lay ready to hand. His life had reached its focal point. He knew already the challenge and something of the complexities of the Chinese society he was to attempt to evangelize; throughout the rest of his long life he was to go on learning and in his turn to pass on his experience and understanding to those who followed him.

Peking itself might be called the Constantinople of the
Chinese Empire, facing outwards towards the barbarians. It is
the north of China which is the most vulnerable. There decisive
battles took place as first the Mongols and then the Tartars
made use of the natural breach afforded by the Pei Ho river to
invade the much coveted kingdom. So Peking was fortified, becoming the seat of the government and, from the beginning of
the fifteenth century, the imperial city.

The new capital was made up of two cities; each a rectangle,
though of different sizes, the wall of one abutting directly on
that of the other. The northern city held the seat of government, and it was surrounded and protected by defensive works
which much engaged Schall's active and practical mind. He
examined the size of the walls, the quality of the materials with
which they were constructed, the number and shape of the
towers and their defensive power. The ramparts were constructed of earth faced with brick and pierced by loopholes.
Some fifteen miles long, they were nearly a hundred feet high,
and on the wide paved top the emperor could drive in his car-
riage or a whole army deploy its forces. There were three hundred and sixty towers, of varying sizes but all of them square.
Schall had criticisms of this uniformity, suggesting that if the
greater towers, of which there were forty-eight at regular intervals, were placed to form an exterior triangular salient the city,
already strong, would be impregnable. Great double gateways,
flanked and surmounted by high buildings, opened to the
north, east and west. In the south, there were three gateways
into the second city of which the middle one was known as the
imperial gate. His detailed study of the city's fortifications was
to be turned to practical account when Schall was later called
upon to give advice on its defence.

The North City, which might be regarded as a fortress of
which the imperial palace was the keep, was itself divided into
further sections, each one with its ramparts. These were the City

of the Officials, the Imperial City and, within it, the Forbidden City; above them, looking down on trees and roofs, rose the shining red walls and golden tiles of the emperor's palace. Here lived the Son of Heaven, inaccessible in god-like mystery and silence. But his semi-divine honours were also chains; he claimed some form of divinity, but it is to be remembered that the usurper always tends to become sooner or later himself enslaved. The emperor was in fact in a prison, his only personal contacts being the eunuchs and ladies of the court. His small world gave some illusion of life and spaciousness through the actual numbers of those who surrounded him. There were three empresses, of whom one took precedence, and two thousand ladies of honour divided into classes according to their prerogatives, with some three thousand waiting women to serve them. As for the eunuchs, there were swarms of these, powerful, proud, and often corrupt.

This monarch ruled a vast empire from his splendid prison. The population has been reckoned at two hundred and fifty million, of whom some fifty-nine million were tax-payers. There were six ministers who held office immediately under the emperor; the minister of the interior (or home secretary), the finance minister, the war minister and the ministers of justice, of public works and of rites (this last office also entailed charge of the highly important Institute of Astronomy). Every morning their reports were presented to the emperor, who handed them on to the Council of State composed of four or five *Kolao* or councillors with a chief councillor at their head. Final decisions rested in the hands of the emperor.

An administration of this kind works very efficiently when the sovereign is markedly capable and gifted; but if he is mediocre or worse it is disastrous. No doubt his subjects ought to be able, and have the right, to depose an incapable ruler; but what in fact happens is that he is kept in power by those who

are in a position to profit by his weakness or incompetence. In
1627 the emperor Wei Chung-hsien died, worn out it may be
supposed with a brief and hectic reign of unusual tyranny and
debauchery. There were no sons, and he was succeeded by his
younger brother, to be known as Ch'ung-chên,[1] a very young
man of ability and good judgment who wished to remedy the
multiple abuses around him. But he had not the necessary
toughness to deal with the unscrupulous vested interests; and
this was to be his downfall. He was the last of the Ming dynasty.

Adam Schall was under no illusions about the physical and
psychological difficulties of approaching the emperor. It was
not only a matter of penetrating the palace, but also of gaining
entry into an almost equally enclosed mind. The way had been
opened and strikingly explored by Schall's great predecessor,
the Jesuit Matthew Ricci, who had come to China in 1583 and
died in Peking in 1610. Effectively the founder of Christian
missionary work in China, Ricci had set out to win interest,
sympathy and, very slowly, conversions by a method novel to
his contemporaries and yet traditional in the life of the Church.
He had worked through a real appreciation of the Chinese way
of life and culture as he found it, and by offering public services
which the highly educated, sometimes suspicious, but also often
genuinely sensitive official Chinese mentality could understand,
respect and make use of. For Schall and his colleague, Father
Giacomo Rho, equally sensitive in understanding the complex
Chinese character, the way of approach, the field of public service, lay in work on the Calendar.

We must understand what the Calendar meant to the
Chinese. It was both popular and scholarly; astrological and
astronomical. While it gave information on the phases of the
moon, eclipses and so on, it provided also a plan or system by

[1] Strictly speaking the title given to his reign; a new emperor took a personal
imperial name and his reign too received a particular appellation; Western
writers have simplified this at the cost of some inaccuracy by using the latter
as if it were a personal name.

which fundamental agricultural life and the work of the community was regulated, and it was furnished besides with picturesque illustrations, stories and a multitude of proverbs and popular sayings. The whole represented for the Chinese a kind of chain linking the Celestial Empire on earth with that of the heavens themselves.

Astrology has of course played a big part in many civilizations, notably those of Egypt, Babylon and Rome among the ancients. This world was seen as a huge organism in which all the interconnected parts, the 'cells', were maintained in being by a ceaseless and mysterious 'give and take' of life. The stars in particular were seen as inexhaustible sources of energy for, and thus influence upon, the earth and men. Men, the microcosms, were governed *en masse* and individually by the world of the stars; while the earth moved in a sort of sympathy with the revolutions of the heavens.

This was very much the Chinese view; but they affirmed more definitely that Heaven or the Heavens (*T'ien*) was a supreme being, from whom, or which, all things were received. Our necessarily vague wording of this statement demonstrates a certain imprecision, typical of the Chinese and foreign to the Western mind (and, of course, unfamiliar to the Christian). All the display of the heavens, the movements of the stars, the phases of the moon, eclipses, the appearance of comets, bore witness to divine wishes which man must understand and carry out if he wants to avoid sickness, war, famine and such like calamities. Nothing of importance was embarked on in public or private life without first consulting the aspect of the stars. The earth would enjoy a reign of peace if its course was ordered by that of the heavens; its prosperity would be secured in proportion to the establishment of harmony between itself and heaven. It was this harmony, a perfect harmony if possible, which it was the Calendar's purpose to bring about. Hence mathematicians and astronomers were engaged in making it as

2

accurate as possible; ideally, of course, perfectly accurate.

This had certainly not yet been achieved. There had been a number of attempts to reform the Calendar, the most notable being in the thirteenth century. Many and alarming mistakes had been made by the official astronomers, due largely to elementary instruments such as the gnomon (an upright rod casting the sun's shadow, as for instance on a sundial), and to too great a dependence on direct observation and on the traditions of centuries. These had proved inadequate for the precise calculation of such things as eclipses and the entry of the sun into the twenty-eight sections of the Chinese zodiac. The first of the Mongol emperors, the famous Kublai Khan, in desperation, called on the science of the Muslim Arabs.[1] They set to work, reforming and innovating. However, the new mathematicians, skilled as they were, inevitably left much to be desired; and by the beginning of the seventeenth century a further reform of the Calendar had become urgent.

Matthew Ricci, with his breadth of mind and freshness of outlook had realized the opportunity thus offered to his Christian mission. Jesuits were of course much involved in the strides being made, we might even say the revolution taking place, in astronomy at the time. With their outstanding education and vigorous, questing minds, as well as their policy of being in the forefront of life in the new world of the post-Reformation and late Renaissance, they studied science and were its teachers. It is often forgotten that the earlier scientist Copernicus was himself in holy orders.

The work of Ricci was the foundation underlying that of Adam Schall, even as Schall's was handed on to Father Ferdinand Verbiest who followed him. Matthew Ricci's life may

[1] This was the basically Greek, above all Ptolemaic, astronomy, preserved by the Arabs and being given back by them to western Europe about this time. See, for instance, *The Divine Comedy* and, in England, the great play Chaucer makes with astronomy in e.g. *The Nun's Priest's Tale*.

be read elsewhere, but we have always to remember that he was 'a great pioneer, point of convergence between East and West, the founder, the model.'[1]

The Jesuits in the Portuguese colony of Macao had been unable to make any sort of impression on the strange Chinese. What were to them the ordinary methods of an apostolate only resulted in misunderstanding and suspicion; they became impatient and, by a common human process developed, as Father Ricci himself remarked, a kind of abhorrence of this stiff-necked people. It was another Italian, Father Alexander Valignano, who was the first to strike a new note, saying among other things that to depend on the power of Portugal or its influence in any way was the sure road to failure with the Chinese. The first thing, of course, was to give up all such ideas. But this had to be followed by some positive fresh approach.

Ricci, having discovered what this might be, makes it clear in a letter dated May 12, 1605, which he wrote to Father John Alvares, assistant to the general of the order for the province of Portugal. Ricci had already had some success in his labours; but he quickly realized that without scientific equipment he lacked an essential tool: 'At the end of this letter,' he writes, 'I repeat insistently a request which I have made before and to which I have had no reply. It would be of the greatest benefit to have at the court [of Peking], a Father or Brother who is an astronomer. I say an astronomer, because I myself know sufficient of geometry, horology and astrolabes and have the necessary books. But the Chinese attach less importance to these than to the movements of the planets, the calculation of eclipses, in fact to the Calendar ... I wish you would take up this most important matter for China with the Father General.' He adds that the task of such a newcomer would be easy enough; the calculations of the Chinese and Arab astronomers contain obvi-

[1] Vincent Cronin, *The Wise Man from the West*, (Rupert Hart-Davis, 1955) p. 264.

ous mistakes, and Ricci himself with the means he had at his disposal had been able to forecast eclipses more precisely than the learned officials. Ricci's view was a wise one. The apostle who was also a good astronomer would gain a hearing, and then respect and gratitude, among all classes of society; he would be seen, such was the Chinese attitude to the Calendar, as a benefactor, perhaps a saviour of the state.

The Call

THIS was the challenge to which Adam Schall responded. What fitted Schall, in particular, for the task? Ricci had been dead some years, the Christian mission was growing if not at the time flourishing, and there were a number of able Jesuits in Peking and scattered over the expanses of the Empire. As we follow Schall's years of often lonely work, with its sometimes startling 'successes' and also its disappointing 'failures', we shall come to a deeper understanding of the temperament and character which made him one of the brilliant figures in the history of Chinese Christianity.

However, first we must look at the earlier life of this young man, priest and Jesuit; our survey will of necessity be fairly brief, as the information is sometimes scanty. It is nevertheless of significance not only in relation to the story of his own life, but as an illustration of the general background of the priests of the Chinese mission: it was by this kind of route that Jesuits of many types and different European nationalities found their way after Matthew Ricci into the Celestial Empire.

John Adam Schall von Bell was born at Cologne on May 1,

1592.[1] His parents, Henry Degenhard von Bell and Mary Scheiffart de Mérode, had two other children, Adam Schall's elder brother, John Reinhard, who became a canon of Hildesheim, and a younger brother, Henry Degenhard. The family had been ennobled in the fourteenth century in the person of Rupert Schall, and had had a distinguished history to which Adam Schall was to add new lustre.

John Adam was endowed with many gifts. He inherited from his family a taste for danger. His insouciance in the face of storms at sea or barbarian Manchus on land recalls the John Schall of the fifteenth century, more adventurer than knight, whose delight it was to make forays with other members of his family from his stronghold at Vorst, near Frechen, into the surrounding countryside, regardless of threats from the city of Cologne. It was such daring, though controlled and disciplined, which inspired his descendant. Thus John Adam's family inheritance was a strength of character and fixity of purpose which could on occasion become obstinacy. He possessed, too, the inexhaustible supply of laughter and jests of the true man of Cologne. But with all his shining, exuberant personality, he was acutely sensitive to other people and vexed by criticism and opposition, on occasion boiling over into some pungent outburst or assailed by languor or melancholy. Here we see the influence of neither family nor city, but of country: Schall was a Rhinelander.

The significant part of Schall's education may be said to begin when, at the age of twelve, he had finished with his primary school, the German *trivialschule* (unless as was often the custom he had had a tutor), and was ready to go on to a 'College of Arts'. There were three in Cologne, the *Montanum*, the *Laurentianum* and the *Tricoronatum*, the last conducted by the Jesuits. The *Tricoronatum* had been founded in 1556 and had flourished in spite of financial troubles and difficulties caused

[1] The date has also been given as 1591, but there now seems no doubt that the following year is correct.

by rival institutions, and by the end of the sixteenth century it was a kind of arsenal of Catholicism. To some Protestants it was known as the *collegium diabolum,* the devil's college, an indication, from whatever point of view, of its prestige and influence. Some thousand pupils studied there, many from German and other noble families. John Adam's parents had clearly been pleased with the solid Christian formation which their eldest son was already receiving, and at the beginning of the academic year of 1604 the younger boy went along with his brother to the college of the Jesuits.

We know practically nothing of this part of the boy's life. The family records have been lost, and there are large gaps in the history of the Jesuits at Cologne just at this time, largely due to the fire on April 4, 1621, which destroyed among the college buildings part of the library, the archives and the chapel. There are a few allusions in letters, some indications in college records. Among Adam's fellows, though a little older, we note the name of Goswin Nickel, a future general of the Society of Jesus. We learn, also, that Adam Schall long remembered the teasing and tormenting (and the feast he had to provide for his tormentors!) which student tradition demanded in their 'baptism' when he graduated. The college authorities waged war on this burlesque ceremony and its accompaniments without success. Of Schall's scholastic gifts and achievements we know only from his pure and even elegant style that he gained a real mastery of classical Latin. There is clearer evidence of Schall's activities in religion. In his second year he became a member of the Congregation of the Holy Angels,[1] being chosen 'assistant' at the beginning of October, 1605, then a councillor

[1] This was a type of Jesuit Sodality. The Sodalities of Our Lady, for men and boys, were founded in 1563 by Father John Leunis S.J.; their objects, like those of other confraternities though a Sodality is more highly organized than many, being the promotion of prayer and retreats among its members and the carrying out of active charitable works.

and secretary on February 19, 1606, finally breathing the rare-
fied air of the 'Parthenica minor'.

A young man of Schall's birth and education had open before
him a wide field: learning, medicine, the army, the priesthood.
In public sermons and private conferences the priesthood
would, of course, have been frequently mentioned. It is also
significant that the director of the Congregation of the Holy
Angels at that time (and for many years) was the very distinguished Father Henry Follaeus of Liège. The tragic state of
Cologne from 1605 may well, also, have impressed a sensitive
mind with the ultimate realities of life. The plague was decimat-
ing the population; striking at random and bringing low human
hopes and plans. The *Tricoronatum* suspended its classes and
closed for three months. In the meanwhile Adam Schall busied
himself with preparations for entering the German College at
Rome, thus following in the footsteps of a relation of his
mother, Hadrian Scheiffart de Mérode, who had died in 1584
at the early age of twenty-five. There he was to meet many of
his fellow-countrymen; but he never returned to Cologne or to
his country. His father, it appears, was already dead; his mother
died in 1621.

At the end of May or the beginning of June 1608, Adam
Schall, accompanied by a man-servant, entered Rome by the
Porta del Popolo and made his way to the German College.
There he presented himself before the vice-rector, Father
Philip Rinaldi (the rector was in Venice) to ask admission to
the College. He was not met with great enthusiasm. The
superior was polite, but it seemed that he was surprised, even
perhaps displeased, to see young Adam. It had been decided
that candidates should not be admitted until they were twenty,
with the exception of young men of noble family who,
according to the Bull of constitution, had the privilege of being
able to present themselves at sixteen. Adam was, then, strictly

speaking of age; but in a letter of April 24 Father Rinaldi had expressly recommended to the vice-rector at Cologne, Father John Léon, that his young protégé should not be sent until he was over seventeen. In a letter to the rector dated June 6 he complains with some vigour about the hasty way in which this candidate had been imposed on them and the embarrassment caused by this child (*tantillus puer*). A ray of sun after this downpour occurs towards the end of the letter where the writer shows his sympathy towards Schall himself: 'The young man makes an excellent impression; but he is really too young, too much of the child' to be admitted.[1] The obstacle was not insurmountable. The auxiliary bishop of Cologne, Duke Ferdinand of Bavaria and nephew of the Prince Elector, was told of the situation by the Jesuit provincial. He in turn interceded with the general, the celebrated Claudio Aquaviva, who was delighted to be able to show his appreciation of the House of Bavaria's benevolence to the Society of Jesus by obtaining the favour.

After the required probation, Schall finally signed the promise to observe the Bull of constitution and the rules of the College on May 24, 1609. In a letter of September 13, Father Rinaldi wrote to Father Copper, the new rector of the *Tricoronatum*, in high praise of the young student. He was, however, rather concerned to see 'the good and noble young man so pale and thin'.

In the midst of his philosophical studies, his delving into the metaphysics of causes, it must be supposed that Schall found himself enamoured of a new ideal: the 'more perfect' way of life and the complete self-giving to God of the religious institute. Among his ancestors there had been Benedictines, Cistercians and Dominicans; and each year he saw some among his fellow students leaving the German College for the Jesuit noviceship, as indeed they still do today. With consultation and

---

[1] The letters are preserved at the German College.

prayer, the idea took root and grew firm; and at the end of his two years' philosophy, he confidently entered the Jesuit noviciate of St Andrew at the Quirinal on October 20, 1611. The German College always retained a special place in his affections. His first letter from the Far East was written to those whom he always thought of as his fellow students; and to the end of his life he remembered with gratitude and affection his old spiritual director, Father James Nusbaum de Dieburg.

Again, we know very little of Schall's years in the noviciate. In October, 1613, he was, according to the custom, caring for the sick in a hospital, either that of the Lateran or the Consolation. A certain soldier persistently refused to make his confession, until Adam exclaimed: 'My patron, the holy Patriarch, help this child who is on the road to perdition!' The following day, we are told, the sinner had a changed outlook. All through his life Schall had this religious attachment to his patron, Adam, often calling on him. In the wearying periods of apparently fruitless work, his constant encouragement was the memory of the laborious, expiatory toil of which Adam, the first of us all, gives the example.

We know also of an incident on a pilgrimage to the church of the Holy Cross at Todi in Umbria. Schall and two companions stayed the night at an inn where certain young travellers were exchanging some pretty dubious jokes amid gales of laughter. Suddenly one of them said: 'There are some Jesuits here!' and that part of the conversation, at least, stopped dead. We are not told of any active part taken by Adam in this; but we do hear that his glance could be extremely effective on occasion.

At the end of October, 1613, the period of the noviceship was over, and Schall went on to the Roman College—the Gregorian University—to follow, and in four years to complete, his theological studies.

On January 2, 1616, he wrote a letter to the general of the Society of Jesus, now Father Mutio Vitelleschi, expressing his hopes of being sent to what was then known as the 'Indies', especially to China. 'I have had this great desire for a long time, since my noviceship,' he says.[1]

Father Matthew Ricci and his successor in China, Father Nicholas Longobardo, had been sending home letters full of their hopes and concerns which may well have opened new horizons to Schall's ever-questing spirit. More than this, in October 1614 Father Nicholas Trigault arrived in Rome on a private mission from Longobardo to the pope. The purpose of this was to set forth the achievements and needs of the mission in China, and more especially to ask for faculties for the establishment of a native clergy. This was granted; and on March 26, 1615, the cardinals of the Holy Office sitting in the presence of Pope Paul V gave formal permission for the mission priests to conform to local custom by saying Mass with their heads covered, for the Bible to be translated into Mandarin (learned or classical Chinese), and authorized future native priests to use their national language for the liturgy, including the Mass. The papal brief was promulgated but, mysteriously and very un-

---

[1] The letter which the young Adam Schall wrote, (in Latin), to Father Vitelleschi with his request to be sent to the East runs like this:

I, Adam Schall, albeit most unworthy, but yet relying on that same goodness of God by which I feel myself called to make this request, here set forth my desire: namely, to go to the East Indies, and especially to China, which I have wanted to do most earnestly for a long time, although it is true that I am still only a novice. After mature reflection, and offering to God many prayers and devotional works for this intention, it seems to me that I should conceal it no longer; so I hereby make my request to the Reverend Father Vitelleschi, following on the spiritual exercises which I have during this time directed to this end. I hope I am not wrong in making this request, for I seem to be greatly impelled to it by the Holy Ghost; and I sincerely avow that I am not stirred by human motives, but rather by desire for God's glory and the salvation of souls. For if I wished to follow human considerations, I would instead return to Germany. But I thought it better to obey God and think that I do so in revealing my vocation . . .

fortunately, the idea of the Chinese liturgy was laid aside and, in spite of later attempts to revive it, never put into practice.

Father Trigault made use of his visit to travel around Europe preaching and appealing for the Chinese mission which needed financial help and, still more, men. A first class speaker as well as a capable writer (his Latin translation of Ricci's memoirs became a highly influential classic), enterprising, bold and tireless, he attracted willing disciples, evoking a sense of mission they hardly knew they possessed. Wherever he went, in Tuscany, France and Flanders, at Trier and Cologne, in Bavaria, Spain and Portugal, alms flowed in and requests to go on the Chinese mission were written off to the general of the Society. Father Trigault launched what can only be called a Chinese movement, whose impetus lasted until the end of the seventeenth century. Thus Adam Schall came into contact with him. At first, indeed, Trigault suggested that Schall should join him on his tour of appeal but, wisely advised, the young man resisted the impulse to immediate activity and decided not to interrupt his studies. But he did write, as we have seen, to the general, and his request was granted. After his ordination, his theological studies completed, Father Schall made all haste to Lisbon there to await Father Trigault. He had to wait some time, as Trigault did not reach the city until February 1618, and it was not until April 16 that the ship, the *Jesus*, with Trigault, Adam Schall and twenty-one other missionaries destined for the Far East on board, weighed anchor.

It was a terrible voyage. The plague struck crew and passengers; on one day there were something like three hundred sick; forty-five of the travellers, including five missionaries, died. In June Schall, exhausted by his work for others, himself fell sick, only to return to his post before he was fully recovered. The epidemic was dying down when mutinies arose among the sailors, the first following the death of the ship's captain on August 24 and the second when food was running short. On both these occasions it was Father Trigault who succeeded in restoring order and peace.

All this, of course, disrupted any regimen of prayer and study; there could be no strict observance of a rule, but at the most an effort to achieve some hours of recollection and reading. Among the missionaries was the brilliant German Swiss scholar, John Terrenz Schreck (commonly known as Terrenz). Born in Switzerland in 1576, he had made a name for himself in Germany as doctor, philosopher and mathematician, being a colleague and a friend, as far as that was possible, of the somewhat irascible Galileo, a friend too of Kepler. In 1611, in the midst of his career, he entered the Society of Jesus, where his scientific learning was to prove valuable. During this voyage, regularly on Tuesdays and Fridays, he gave his companions a course in mathematics. Adam Schall must have been one of his most diligent pupils. Later on, when we find Schall himself demonstrating his mastery of such learning, the question may be asked as to where he had acquired the knowledge he was teaching, and there is no very satisfactory reply. This course of Father Terrenz's supplies at least part of the answer; he may have been the first, he must certainly have been the most distinguished of Father Schall's masters in science.

It is said that time passes swiftly when one is busy; the missionaries were indeed kept occupied one way and another. In fact, also, the voyage was a fast one. The *Jesus* entered the port of Goa on October 4, 1618, having taken five and a half months instead of the more usual seven. Father Schall ascribed this to the intercession of the saints of Cologne and Trier, relics of whom the travellers carried with them.

In Goa, often in those days optimistically dubbed the Rome of Asia, the missionaries remained for some months. During this time, from November 24 to January 11, the courses of two comets were visible. These were observed by Schall and Father Wenceslaus Pantaleon Kirwitzer, a Bohemian who had been

teaching mathematics at the Jesuit College at Graz when
Father Trigault attracted him to the China mission. Father Kirwitzer died at Macao on May 22, 1626, after having done good
work in China. A little later, on January 25, Schall was present
at an imposing ceremony in the church of St Paul when the
Bishop of Japan baptized seven hundred catechumens, whose
godparents included the viceroy himself and others of the
nobility. In his letter of February 9, 1619, Father Schall tells
the students of the German College what he has been seeing and
hearing, revealing those qualities which were always to remain
his: shrewd observation coupled with a certain simplicity. He
remarks the indolence of the Portuguese and its contrast with
the busyness of the Dutch and the English; he is interested in
the discovery of silver mines near the Zambezi, and records,
quite seriously, the report that the Great Mogul has mustered
fifteen thousand elephants and three hundred thousand horses
in his preparations for war against the Persians.

In the meantime, the group of missionaries, already reduced
in number by the plague, diminished still further. On December
6, 1618, Elias, Nicholas Trigault's brother, died, his death possibly hastened by his magnificent work for the sick on board the
Jesus; and he was soon followed by the Brother, Gonzalo Dias.
Some Fathers, moreover, who were originally meant for China
went to other missions. Of those who set out in the first place
there were now eight left. These were: Francis Furtado from
the Azores, who was to be at the head of the vice-province of
China for many years; John Froes, a Portuguese, who remained
in Goa for some time, only reaching China in 1624; Simon da
Cunha, also Portuguese, who did not reach Macao until 1624
and entered China in 1629, where he became at one time and
another both vice-provincial and visitor apostolic, dying at
Macao in 1660, and Nicholas Trigault, Giacomo Rho, Terrenz,
Kirwitzer and Schall.

The stay in Goa seemed to be lasting rather a long time. Towards the end of 1618, the visitor apostolic to the Far East urged Nicholas Trigault to set out for Macao without further delay, though he had to exercise patience until May 20, 1619, when Trigault and Terrenz took ship for Macao, arriving there on July 22. Schall and Kirwitzer left a little later, and had an adventurous voyage. In the Malacca Strait the ship was over-taken by a storm and ran onto a sand-bank. It seemed impossible to re-float her, even after some of the cargo had been jettisoned. Then the two missionaries called to mind that they carried with them relics of the Eleven Thousand Virgins, the companions of St Ursula who, according to the legend, were martyred at Cologne. These they brought on deck, invoking the intercession of the saints, and lo and behold! the ship was free and able to sail on her way. In the South China Sea they ran into another storm which raged for three days and nights; even so, they sighted Macao on July 15, 1619.

We may guess at Adam Schall's thoughts as they made towards the great amphitheatre of Macao after fourteen months on the journey. Macao was the port and gateway to China, that mysterious, unyielding country, with its millions of souls in need of deliverance from the 'Chinese dragon'; an immense field of labour, in which the good worker might dream of a harvest of a hundredfold, though his task could well be to sow, or even simply to plough the virgin ground. The work was to be done, and God would give the increase; but as the ship slipped quietly into the embracing arms of the harbour, eagerness may have been shot through with a certain trepidation.

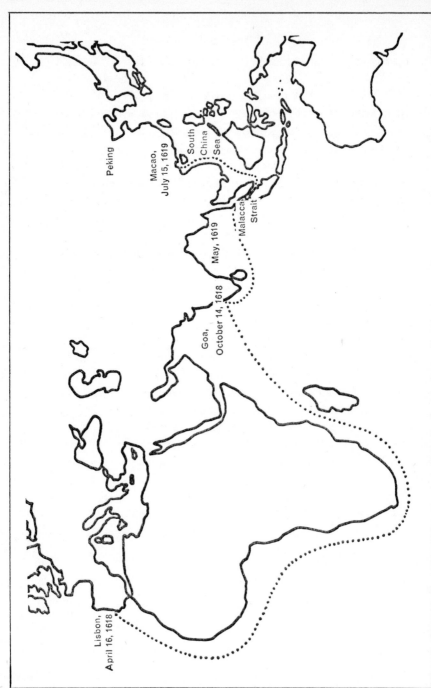

Peking

Macao,
July 15, 1619

South
China
Sea

Malacca
Strait

May, 1619

Goa,
October 14, 1618

Lisbon,
April 16, 1618

Map I. Showing Schall's journey from Europe

Waiting at Macao

M ACAO was a Portuguese colony. Its physical proximity
to China could be highly misleading. Father Schall
waited at Macao for three years while the various
'Chinese walls' which stood between him and his destination
were surmounted. There was already bad news of persecution
of Christians; and Schall was to learn, moreover, that in China
nothing could be hurried.

Public affairs were much troubled; the Emperor, Wan-li,
took his ease behind a sort of defence-work of courtesans and
palace eunuchs and, unhappily, missionaries were also at fault.
The vice-president of the Board of Rites, or Ceremonies, at
Nanking (the 'Capital of the South': the older and more beautiful city, Peking, the seat of the imperial court, was the 'Capital
of the North') had determined to wipe out Christianity.

The counsels of Father Matthew Ricci had not been wholly
followed. Until the time of his death in 1610, he had constantly
impressed the need for discretion and prudence on his fellow-
workers, saying that one blunder could destroy all their
achievements; not by attempting to forestall his providence was
God's work to be carried on speedily and surely. This advice

3

was approved by such men as the Chinese Christian scholars Paul Hsü Kuang-ch'i, Leo Li Chih-tsao and Michael Yang T'ing-yün; but others found it uncongenial. Among the missionaries, Father Longobardo and Father Alfonso Vagnoni for instance, felt in their optimism that this wisdom was timidity, that what was recommended as prudent delay was in fact hanging back. The time had come for publishing the Gospel not only openly but resoundingly in China.

Father Vagnoni at Nanking had built a church in the western style, giving its ceremonies and celebrations the greatest publicity. Father Longobardo, it appears, even thought of petitioning the emperor for an edict of full Christian liberty. Christian mandarins (scholar-officials) were unanimous in their disapproval of such a step. The eminent Paul Hsü Kuang-ch'i, who had been a friend of Matthew Ricci and is 'rightly regarded as the greatest glory of Chinese Catholicism',[1] in particular opposed an illusion which he knew was dangerous and should at all costs be discarded. He emphasized that every time he had taken part in the deliberations of the supreme council of the empire there had been discussion on how to turn the Portuguese out of Macao; and that in one year alone three petitions had been addressed to the imperial court asking that the (Jesuit) Fathers, the emissaries of Portugal, should be sent home.

Father Longobardo's idea was apparently dropped; but such words of moderation were already too late. There were protests against the missionaries' ostentatious ceremonies and public preaching; hostile feeling grew up among the people. The new vice-president of the Board of Rites in Nanking, Shên Ch'üeh, was an ambitious man who had as well a personal antagonism against such distinguished Chinese Christian mandarins as Paul Hsü Kuang-ch'i and Michael Yang T'ing-yün. But it must also be remembered that he was a leader of Sung orthodoxy; that is, he represented an embedded and long

[1] George H. Dunne S.J., *Generation of Giants*, (Burns & Oates, 1962) pp. 67-8.

favoured state religion to which Christianity was an insult if not a threat. In May 1616, he addressed his first accusation to the imperial court at Peking: 'The Fathers claim to make known the religion of the Lord of Heaven who reigns over the whole world, whereas the Emperor is the Master of all things. They have the impudence to settle the courses of the stars and to forbid the offering of sacrifices to our ancestors.' The document, which is well presented, is also double-faced. The ambiguous Chinese characters in this quotation can also be taken as reading: 'The foreign dogs, propagators of a pernicious doctrine, wish to destroy the rule of the Emperor whom Heaven itself has made lord; they stir up rebellion and allow their officials to do as they like.' The conclusion follows of itself, though Shên Ch'üeh only makes the suggestion: send the foreigners eighty thousand *Li* away; confiscate their books; set up an enquiry to find out exactly when the missionaries arrived in China and their precise numbers, and track down those who have given them support: 'Then peace will reign for ten thousand times ten thousand years.'

Shên waited vainly for a reply, and then returned to the charge, with the support of the president of the Board of Rites. The president took action on his own responsibility at the end of August, and finally the imperial signature was obtained to an edict of condemnation and banishment on February 14, 1617, which was promulgated throughout the empire. Father Diego de Pantoia, a Spaniard who had worked with Ricci and had been in Peking for sixteen years, and Father Sebastian de Ursis from the Kingdom of Naples, who had been in Peking for eleven years, another close companion of Ricci's, were banished. They both died in exile in Macao. It is fairly typical of the Chinese system and mentality that Father Longobardo, for instance, not being actually mentioned by name in the imperial edict was passed over by the officials carrying it out. Father Vagnoni and the Portuguese Father Alvaro Semedo were banished from

Nanking. Less fortunate than de Pantoia and de Ursis, they were brought before Shên himself in Nanking and sentenced to ten blows of the bastinado—the common Chinese penalty administered with a bamboo cane to the feet. Semedo tells us that Father Vagnoni's wounds took a month to heal, but that he himself in fact escaped the punishment because he was at that time seriously ill. They were finally sent out of the city in cages —usually reserved for criminals condemned to death—and a long journey, its many sufferings relieved by consolations from the support of fellow Christians and sympathizers, brought them to Macao.[1] Both Fathers in due course returned to imperial China.

The remaining missionaries kept their spirits up and continued with their work. This was made no easier by a period of confusion increased by the death of the Emperor Wan-li, and in which Shên Ch'üeh played a notable part. Secret societies were always liable to appear in China, especially in times of public unrest, and Christians underwent considerable sufferings when they were accused of association with the White Lotus Society which was causing a good deal of trouble. In 1662, however, Shên was first called to Peking to become grand secretary and then almost at once fell decisively from favour

[1] This is Father Semedo's account of his and Father Vagnoni's expulsion from Nanking and part of the journey:

They put us in very narrow wooden cages, with chains round our necks, our feet in irons, our hair uncut and our clothes disordered, to show that we were foreigners and barbarians; and thus confined like wild animals we were, on April 30, 1617, taken from the prison to a court in order that imperial seals might be affixed to the cages. Three big notice boards were carried before us, with our sentence written out in large characters and a warning to all Chinese to have nothing to do with us. In this manner we left Nanking, remaining in our cages, and after a month we came to the chief city of the province of Canton and were brought before the governor. After sharply reproving us for having presumed to preach a new law in China, he handed us over to some mandarins who trailed us from court to court followed by extraordinary crowds of people. Then we were thrust outside the city to resume our journey to Macao, which we reached after some days.

through the hostility of his own enemies. He died in his home in Hangchow two years later. The mission was saved from further active persecution.

When Father Schall reached Macao in July, 1619, the persecution was at its height, the mission threatened and the work of the missionaries seriously endangered. This must have been the great subject of conversation among the sixty to eighty Jesuits, six of them of the Chinese mission, who made up the community there. Everyone would have had his say about past misfortunes and fears for the future. There was much here that a new arrival could learn and take to heart, and not only the particulars of the work and sufferings of the exiled Fathers. Father Vagnoni introduced him to the mysteries of the Chinese language; and also, no doubt in a way he did not himself fully realize, to the mysteries of the Chinese mind. The exploits of this priest and his companions, with their only too striking consequences, revealed the difficulties and demands of this missionary field. If a thousand years are as a day in the sight of God so are they, too, in Chinese eyes. Deep in their age-old traditions, the Chinese were not to be hurried; unseemly haste meant loss of face in a country where the shortest distance from one point to another was not a straight line.

In June, 1622, a new danger threatened, this time not from hostile Chinese but from the Dutch who had settled in Java and Sumatra. Today, Macao is a pleasant estuary always in danger of silting up, the town full of religious houses but with little organic life; its revenue is said to be derived mainly from such things as gambling houses and opium and it bears its proportion of the burden and disruptive influences of refugees. Its great rival for trade and position, Hong Kong, across the water, triumphed in 1842. In 1622, however, built in a kind of amphitheatre on a rocky peninsula in the south west of China, its position was such that Portugal could well say that Macao was its strongest foothold in the East. The port promised its possessor a monopoly of trade with Japan, the Moluccas and China.

The Dutch knew this well enough and had hopes of seizing Macao; the more so since 1604 when their envoy, Wybrand van Warwick, had failed to negotiate a trading agreement with China at Canton. Strong in their position, the Portuguese had been able to use their influence against such an agreement. In 1600 and 1603 and again in 1607 a Dutch fleet had made its appearance off Macao and captured heavily-laden Portuguese vessels. After 1609 there was a lull: Holland and Spain (with whom Portugal had been politically united since 1580) agreed to a twelve year truce.

In Macao the time was used, with some foresight, to put up fortifications. Even so, the town had little in the way of armaments, except for six cannon obtained from Manila. Four of these, though reckoned obsolete, were, thanks to Father Bruno the acting superior, mounted on the hill where the Jesuit college stood.

On June 22, 1622, thirteen Dutch ships (with two English standing by) blocked the entrance to the port; and next day three of them made an attack on the fort of San Francisco, which failed. The virtually undefended isthmus of Casilha next attracted the attention of the Dutch admiral, Cornelis Reijersen, who decided to land on the east bank where there was nothing to deter him except a few fishermen's huts and some hastily thrown-up earthworks. On the 24th a bombardment demolished these bulwarks, scattered the handful of men posted on the hill of Guya and the landing began. The Dutch commander, Reyertz, fell, struck by a musket ball, but the attack continued with two companies bringing ashore cannon and munitions. Confident of victory, the army marched towards the town now wide open to them from this quarter, with flags flying and the martial music of pipe and drum. But there was the sound of gunfire from the Jesuit college on the hill; four cannon only, with very few balls to fire, but they had the advantage of complete surprise. The startled Dutch instinctively recoiled to take refuge behind a hillock on their left, and this was the signal for the people of Macao, spurred on apparently by the drum-beats of Father Bruno as well as the example of their commander, Lopo Sarmento de Carvalho, to fall on the Dutch. Among the Jesuits and friars who took part in the fray was Adam Schall, who succeeded in capturing a Dutch captain. The enemy took to their heels and made for their boats; such was their panic that a good proportion of their losses were from drowning as the men struggled in the sea.

The Portuguese in the East celebrated the victory of Macao with bonfires and processions of thanksgiving. The rejoicing of the Fathers was less for political or nationalistic reasons than for the preservation of Catholicism in Macao, which illuminates the rather striking part they played in the battle. The conquest of Macao by the Dutch would have meant not only the supremacy of Dutch trade in China but also of Dutch Calvinism; Catholicism would have had to go underground and the Chinese mission would have been isolated. Hence we see Jesuits, transformed very nearly into soldiers, facing a common enemy with the Portuguese traders, though for not precisely similar reasons. The modern mind which tends to be made uneasy by this sort of situation is not always equally sensitive to the customs and attitudes of other times; nor do we do well to forget that the conception of taking up arms in a moral or, as some saw it, even a religious cause was once again largely accepted and even proclaimed in the Second World War. (Our judgment of the principle involved is too often swayed by our sympathy or lack of sympathy with the particular circumstances.) Certainly men like Schall (himself no Portuguese) knew well enough the difference between what was for them the cause of Christ and the political and trading ambitions of Portugal. In fact, this question of active participation in defence of the state was to be forced on Schall much more directly later on, and he was by no means happy about it then.

Patient Beginnings

FTER three long years of waiting, Adam Schall was very ready for his mission. Through his study of the language that had such beautiful characters and such differing basic concepts from the tongues of the West, he was gaining an insight into the complexities of the Chinese mind and a comprehension that there could be no entry for the West as such into the Celestial Empire. For a long time now he had left behind relatives, country and familiar ways; even the very recent noise of battle and smell of gunpowder sank into insignificance. He had learned from the accounts and experiences of the exiled Fathers, from the persecution, occasioned by suspicion and often hatred of the foreigner, which was exacerbated by the tactless and in Chinese eyes impudent behaviour of the Christians, that to preach Christ to the Chinese the man of the West must himself become a Chinese. The real reason for this lay in the mind; but the Chinese were too formal and civilized a people to regard the exterior of a man, in our modern manner, as of accidental interest or importance, and Schall was henceforth to dress as a Chinese, to be the more readily accepted by those he was to work among. There was in fact no difficulty as far as

clothes went: the Jesuit missionaries had realized the necessity
of not appearing foreigners to outward view. At first they had
adopted what might seem the sensible custom of wearing the
dress of the Buddhist monks, but Matthew Ricci gradually came
to the conclusion that this was unsatisfactory; the Christian
priests were all too often actually taken for Buddhist priests,
who were, moreover, frequently lax and ignorant. He adopted,
then, the silk robes and tall 'hat' of the Chinese scholar, in this
way making plain his claims to learning and to teach wisdom,
and smoothing the path of prickly Chinese etiquette in necessary
and valuable relations with officials and other important men.
This then became the normal dress of the Jesuit missionary;
though there were occasions when it was deemed advisable to
put on simpler, humbler Chinese costume. Their hair, which
had earlier been shaven like that of the Buddhist monks, was
now grown long in accordance with the custom of the educated
Chinese, though it was normally taken up neatly under the
headdress.

Names also play an important role in Chinese life and the
missionaries adopted Chinese names. If it is true that a man
feels his identity in some way intimately bound up with his name,
then it must have been a final emptying of the European Adam
Schall henceforth to call himself, and be addressed as, T'ang
Jo-wang.

Towards the end of 1622, Schall left Macao for Peking. On
the way he was joined by Father Longobardo who had just been
succeeded as superior of the mission by Father da Rocha, another of Ricci's fellow-workers. Da Rocha was to be appointed
first vice-provincial of the Jesuit order in China later, when the
status of the mission was raised to that of a province, but he
died in 1623 before word of this even reached him.

On January 25, six days after the celebration of the Chinese
New Year, the two travellers arrived in Peking and made their
way to the house established by Father Ricci in 1605 in the

North City, near its south-western gate. The Christian community was not at its most vigorous. The edict of expulsion promulgated against the Jesuits during the recent persecution had not in fact yet been revoked, leaving them in a rather ambiguous position. Prudence and discretion were the order of the day: attributes not at all to the taste of enthusiastic new missionaries. The Christian mandarins, conscious of this insecurity, sought to obtain official permission for the Fathers to remain. A Chinese is never at a loss. The government was anxious about the movement of Manchu troops on the border and had some fears of an invasion; so the Christian mandarins blandly proposed to the interested officials the invaluable aid of those military experts, Father Longobardo and Father Manoel Dias (known as 'the younger'). The game was solemnly played out on both sides; the offer was accepted though never acted on, and the Jesuits were given official permission to stay on.

Adam Schall was quick to take advantage of the liberty thus won to make contact with those around him. The intellectual curiosity natural to the Chinese came to his aid. He drew up a list of the mathematical and astronomical works he had brought from Europe and had this presented at the imperial court. He carefully demonstrated his apparatus and how to use it to the many interested people who came to see. The minister of finance himself took an interest in these new things, and having assured himself of the Jesuit's scientific attainments became his warm supporter, indeed his friend.

An eclipse of the moon was forecast for October 8, 1623. The minister made himself familiar with Schall's calculations, which proved strictly accurate when the time came. The following day, the minister, escorted by various officials, presented himself to congratulate Schall and moreover to ask, according to polite Chinese custom, to be accepted as his pupil. He announced to his companions: 'In this century China has been able to congratulate herself on the possession of two men remarkable for their science and their virtue: Father Ricci and this, our master.' He then requested that his master would be so good as to make the calculations for a lunar eclipse, forecast for September of the following year, and present them to him. This Schall promised to do; but he modestly and prudently declined the honour of treating the minister as his pupil. He set to work at once, and thus composed his first scientific work—a book of two small volumes which, while determining the exact time of the eclipse, also described its whole course. Schall was invited to the minister's house to watch the event, and once again his forecasts were fulfilled. The delighted mandarin wanted to obtain a state salary for Schall, but the Jesuit judged this to be rather premature.

The talents and early success shown here seem to indicate a new Matthew Ricci. But his superiors at the mission did not look on Schall and his enterprises with a particularly favourable eye. It was still relatively early in the experience of the mission, and Ricci's methods were too original to receive universal approbation. His successors, de Pantoia and de Ursis, had been exiled from Peking in the persecution and with them Jesuit astronomical studies had gone too. Why, then, risk the unleashing of more troubles on the still suspect community by showing an interest in that recurrent question the reform of the official Chinese Calendar? The finance minister and a few others might favour the idea; but no request had been made from an official source. This was thought to be the realistic view; but Schall had a sense of realities too. Convinced of the essential importance of astronomy, so dear to the Chinese mind, in the future work of the mission, he quietly applied himself to his studies and bided his time.

1625 and 1626 were, then, years of study for Schall and for Father Terrenz, too. They had, among other things, to perfect their knowledge of the language, which it is probable they did under the instruction of Paul Hsü Kuang-ch'i.

Schall was regarded as having good but not outstanding qualities. We can still read his superiors' estimation of him: he has ability and intelligence; he is progressing well in Chinese studies; his excellent nature, his joviality and friendliness are notable, but he lacks ballast and maturity; in short, he is not fitted, at least as yet, to be in a position of authority. Schall in fact never would have been the diplomat, weighing each word and action and its likely consequences; he could be imprudent, though this was through finding other things more important in given circumstances, rather than from any contempt for prudence itself. But he was certainly not cut out to be the superior of a group of religious, whose first care and constant task has to be the serenity and good-ordering of his house with its varying needs and personalities. His qualities were those of the pioneer: quickness to apprehend a situation, boldness to take advantage of it, a generous temperament making him popular or at least acceptable, and the tenacity to complete his work. The occasion had not yet arisen for these gifts to shine; and his particular faults were those most conspicuous to timid or judicious minds already irritated by his outbursts of boisterous humour. Schall was doubtless thought to be too free and too critical; his superiors did not share the admiration of the Chinese finance minister who called him 'master'. Consequently, perhaps a brake was put upon Schall's enterprises which involved methods and matters which he so strongly believed in. Certainly towards the end of the year 1627, Schall was sent to Sianfu, the capital of the province of Shensi.

Sianfu—commonly known as Sian—was a famous city. It had been the seat of the early dynasties, a focus for the ambitions of warriors and merchants alike. When he saw it rising up before him in the valley of the Wei Ho, the cradle of Chinese civilization, Schall remembering his *Anabasis* could have exclaimed with Xenophon: 'O beautiful and gorgeous city!' It was indeed imposing and splendid, with its fourteen miles of

square-built battlements and four monumental gateways surmounted by tiers of lodges or 'pavilions', its palaces and great
houses, all recalling the glory of the ancient capital. Nothing
now remains of what was then spread before the admiring eyes
of Schall; Sianfu today is a small town of humble peasant
dwellings.

There had been an unsuccessful visit by missionaries to the
province of Shensi in 1619, followed by a more fruitful mission
in 1621 when Father Giulio Aleni went there accompanied by
Peter Ma San-chih, a scholar and official of the Shensi province
whom Aleni had first instructed in Western mathematics and
then baptized.[1] A little after this Father Nicholas Trigault had
visited Sian itself, and it was Schall's task firmly to establish
and encourage the tiny mission. In this far from easy charge
he was fortunate in being able to count on the support and aid
of two scholars who had already done much for Father Trigault: Philip Wang Chêng and Paul Chang Chung-fang. In
Sianfu, Wang Chêng bought a good house which was to be the
residence of Schall and his colleague Father Semedo, and the
two set valiantly to work. They were met, however, by ill-will
and opposition which did not hesitate at abuse, slander and even
blows. 'The prisons of Nanking were more tolerable,' declared
Father Semedo, who knew something about it. Their labours
seemed to be bearing little fruit and Semedo was transferred.

Schall, remaining in Sianfu alone, did not lose heart. He was
of that temperament whose courage and vigour rise in proportion to the challenge. Attacking the problem face on, he built a
chapel, with financial help from his benefactor Wang Chêng,
and dedicated it to the Mother of God. Soon afterwards he
dared even further and was responsible for something much

[1] It was near Sian in 1625 that the famous Nestorian inscribed tablet was
discovered by workmen. Educated Chinese and Jesuits alike took a profound
interest in this evidence of a flourishing eighth-century Christian community
in China; though for a long time anti-Jesuits, anti-Catholics or anti-
Christians in Europe regarded it as a 'typical' piece of Jesuit falsehood.

more like a full-scale church; the chapel was now reserved for the use of Christian women—thus attempting to deal with the thorny question of Chinese sensitivity over social relations with women and the missionaries' contacts with them. At the same time, Father Schall was experiencing the benefits of a general softening of the attitude towards the Christian missionaries throughout the empire, deriving from political changes in Peking. The building of the church became a centre of interest. A neighbour of Schall's, a personage both influential and originally hostile, consented to superintend the masons; and when all was finished sightseers flooded in. They wondered especially at the gilded cross rising above the roof and, inside, at the statue of Christ which appeared to smile on all those who came before it. The new attitude on the part of the officials was strikingly demonstrated by the action of the viceroy who presented Schall with a *pai-pien*, a formal eulogy, praising Western science and Schall and his colleagues as representatives of it. The immediate fruit of all this was fifty baptisms; a large number at that time and place.

Schall was interesting himself also in a geographical problem. The sea route to China was long, hard and often dangerous. Since Ricci's time the question had been raised as to the possibility of avoiding some of these difficulties by making the long trek overland. Schall was well placed for investigating this question from the Chinese end as Sian, a trading centre, was the terminus of the ancient and famous caravan route through central Asia via Bokhara and Suchow. Most of this trail had in fact once been followed by a Jesuit Brother, Bento de Goes, who accompanied a caravan from Lahore; a four years' journey of frequent dangers and great interest. De Goes had died in Suchow in 1607, having managed to get in touch with Ricci in Peking, who was able to send a Chinese Jesuit Brother to his aid. The importance of this journey had lain not in any definite idea of mapping out a regular overland route for people from the West, but in clarifying the till then extremely obscure question of the relationship between the Cathay described so vividly and impressively by Marco Polo and the China now known to the Jesuit missionaries. That they were one and the same was made clear by the simple fact that de Goes had traversed the country in between, including that area where Cathay had been supposed to be situated, and there was no sign of anything that could be the land of Marco Polo's explorations. Schall set himself to discover and examine all the evidence that he could obtain, consulting those learned in geography and taking full advantage of the caravans which arrived at periodic intervals according to the regulations of entry into the Empire. Among the travellers, merchants and foreign envoys (these latter a face-saving necessity, bringing 'tribute' to the emperor himself) with whom he talked was the Muslim leader of a large caravan which arrived in Sian in 1628. The two men found they were developing what must have appeared on either side a most unlikely friendship, and many visits were exchanged before the caravan leader, Mirjudin, moved on to Peking. Schall had his discussions with other members of this caravan too, and in the following year he wrote the account of his findings. In this he confirms the identification of Cathay with China for the benefit of the few who still doubted it, noting that on the old maps Cathay was placed too far to the north and that Marco Polo's Khanbaligh was indeed, as Ricci had maintained, Peking. He gives much careful information about the caravan routes, and also informs us that a journey from Aleppo to Suchow would take three hundred and twenty-five days. The overland route was no nearer, however, to being a practical proposition.

Among other things with which Schall busied himself were the determination of the latitude of Sianfu and the exact calculation of the eclipse of the moon on January 21, 1628. He also translated lives of the saints into Chinese to please Philip Wang Chêng, who saw to it that the robes of a Chinese scholar which

Schall wore should be absolutely correct when the author presented the work in public.

At this time there was considerable discussion among the missionaries over the problem of translating theological terms into Chinese. The use of a language in which Christian terms have to be expressed quite freshly from the start is always difficult; this difficulty is inescapable, since however finely shades of theological meaning may be expressed in Latin (or in Greek, both once themselves 'pagan languages' whose genius was pressed into Christian use), Christian teaching and writing has to start in the vernacular with such essential words and concepts as 'God'. The missionaries in China were exercised over the variety and subtlety of the Chinese language; afraid, in a way that was not perhaps altogether true to the spirit of primitive times or so familiar to us today with our attempts to enlarge our vision of the role of non-Christian religions, of too great an intermingling of old pagan attitudes in Christian concepts. It would seem, too, that they did not fully realize that Chinese linguistic subtlety did not lead and was not intended to lead to greater and greater precision of language and thought; rather, it made room for a good deal of latitude and flexibility— vagueness, the Westerner might call it on occasion.

It was the term 'God' which in fact raised the problem in acute form. There were four possible words to make use of when referring to the Supreme Being: *T'ien*—The Heavens; *T'ien-chu*—The Lord of the Heavens; *Shang-ti*—Highest Ruler, and *Teusu* which is simply *Deus* made as Chinese as possible (as if for instance some form of this Latin word had been presented by St Augustine to the Anglo-Saxon peoples of England for use in daily life rather than adopting their word *god*.)

Father Vagnoni favoured *Shang-ti*; *T'ien* he tolerated at most. Father Longobardo was firm in his recommendation of *Teusu*, even *T'ien-chu* he viewed with suspicion. There had

4

Map II. Map of China, showing places mentioned in text.

been lively discussions both before and since a conference which considered the question at Macao in 1621; and again a conference was held, this time in 1628 in Kiating, near Shanghai, where there was a small Jesuit house of studies. The younger Father Dias, now vice-provincial, presided over some vigorous debates. This conference considered also a number of related matters, such as the question of the honour paid by the Chinese to Confucius and to their ancestors; were these rites harmless civil or 'natural' customs or were they to be regarded as religious in the exact sense and therefore idolatrous? The general agreement here was that there was nothing clearly idolatrous about them, and the Jesuits continued at least to tolerate them as they had done before. Schall appears to have been of the same opinion, or at least to have accepted it, though he did not take an active part in the conference. We do know however that he was not in favour of the use of the term *Shang-ti* for Almighty God. The controversy was hottest and longest over the question of terminology. It continued well after this meeting, showing that a variety of terms were still in active use. In fact, it was finally *T'ien-chu* which became the word used by Chinese Catholics in our sense of God, and is still so today.

Father Schall had made a start in his missionary work. At the same time Sianfu had revealed Schall to his superiors. They realized more fully the uncommon character, the tenacity which tempered and strengthened the enthusiasm under that jovial, almost free and easy exterior. On July 31, 1628, Adam Schall made his final vows as a member of the Society of Jesus. The father general delegated Father Semedo to receive those vows, he who of all people knew best what Adam Schall had contended with and how much he had achieved.

Some two years later Schall was recalled to Peking, where new work awaited him. Sian might have put on mourning at his departure, but to the officials of the place it was professional advancement and therefore an occasion for congratulation and honours. Provisions, a litter and pack animals were offered Schall for the journey, while the officials of the districts through which he would pass were instructed to come out to meet and escort him. Whatever Adam Schall may have felt about it, it must have been something very like a triumphal march.

Peking 1630-1641

So John Adam Schall came once more to Peking. Now the Chinese authorities were again willing to listen to the advice of the European scientists. As we saw, Father de Pantoia and Father de Ursis, who had carried on Ricci's astronomical work in the midst of much hostility from their Chinese 'rivals', had been exiled in the persecution of 1617. But although Chinese astronomers could supplant the Fathers, they could not take their place; they stood in need of their learning. This became clear in 1629 when another eclipse of the moon was forecast. The emperor Ch'ung-chên, vexed with his astronomers, drew their attention sharply to its importance and threatened punishment if they made a mistake this time. This warning could hardly keep them from error, and the emperor's confidence in Chinese and Arab science was seriously shaken. This was the opportunity for the Christian mandarin, Paul Hsü Kuang-ch'i, now vice-president of the Board of Rites, to try to bring about a new entry for the Fathers into official astronomy. He had observed the eclipse himself and been able to judge Father Terrenz's accuracy. 'It is not the culpable ignorance of the Chinese astronomers but their system which is at fault;

53

only the Europeans can remedy these errors for us,' he told the
emperor. As witness to his words, he had a copy of Father
Schall's dissertation on the eclipses of the sun and moon sent to
all the interested authorities. The emperor signified his
approval, adding: 'I know well that the first emperor of our
dynasty had the desire to correct the Calendar ... War pre-
vented the execution or at least the achievement of his purpose.
Let your board do everything that is required and see that we
are informed of all that takes place.' Hsü Kuang-ch'i promptly
called upon Father Terrenz and Father Longobardo, whom he
had long had in mind, and did everything he could to make their
task easier: improved instruments were made according to their
instructions, European mathematical and astronomical books
were to be translated, and, as with de Pantoia and de Ursis before their exile, financial maintenance was to be provided. But
hardly had he begun his work than the brilliant Father Terrenz
died on May 13, 1630. In an edict of September 27, 1629, the
emperor had expressly charged the vice-president of the Board
of Rites with the reform of the Calendar, approving the employ-
ment of the Jesuits. Hsü Kuang-ch'i, therefore, at once nomina-
ted two (always of course with the emperor's permission) to
take Terrenz's place: Father Schall, Terrenz's pupil, and
Father Rho. By the autumn of 1630, Adam Schall had entered
on his official duties.

These duties gave him, and the missionaries at large, a
greatly improved standing. They were also onerous. It was not
simply a matter of astronomical accomplishments; there was a
different and complex chronology to untangle but not to destroy.
The Chinese system reckoned from the year 2697 before Christ,
which was the first of the reign of the possibly legendary emperor, Huang Ti. From this they measured in cycles of sixty
years, and the years themselves were subdivided into months,
days and hours in groups of sixty.

A Chinese year, which was identified by a name, was calcu-

lated from the combination of the movements of the sun and the
moon. It contained twelve months of twenty-nine or thirty days
which began at the new moon. The ever-increasing discrepancy
thus produced was complicated every nineteen years by additional (intercalary) months which took the name of the month
they were intended to prolong. The first month of the astronomical year was reckoned from the winter equinox; but the
beginning of the state year depended on the choice of the emperor, it usually being the third astronomical month.

The day, the interval of time proceeding from minute to
minute, every four equivalent to a solar degree, was divided into
a hundred equal parts called *K'o*. An hour was made up of $8\frac{1}{3}$
K'o; thus dividing the day into twelve hours each equal to two
Western hours.

This gives a slight notion of the kind of problem Schall and
Rho had to deal with. The Calendar alone, with its unique place
in the history of the empire and the reigns of the emperors and
the traditions and customs handed down from ancient times,
demanded enormous erudition and application.

They began their task, while Hsü Kuang-ch'i enabled them
to open and fit up a kind of centre of studies where Chinese
Christian students were trained in mathematics and astronomy
and were set to work translating various European texts. This
ever active friend also presented to the emperor translations
made almost at once by the Fathers themselves, himself revis-
ing their style so that they might be couched in the most acceptable Chinese literary manner. By 1635 there were already a
hundred and fifty small volumes, catalogued in three sections:
auxiliary sciences, theory and practice of astronomy, and astronomical tables. In order to facilitate the use of such European
works and with the advantages of the Gregorian calendar in
mind (though knowing well that it could not be introduced in
their time), the Jesuit scholars divided the day into 96 parts,
the hour then into 8 instead of $8\frac{1}{3}$ parts, and the course of the

sun into the normal Western 360 degrees instead of $365\frac{1}{4}$.

In February 1634, the Fathers had a telescope conveyed to the emperor; and in August this was followed by a celestial globe, an armillary sphere (a celestial globe consisting of a hollow sphere constructed of the astronomical circles) and a sundial. This last, says Schall with some pride, was made of a slab of fine white marble five feet wide; the gnomon was prettily held by a golden dragon. Such attentions merited a reward: the Fathers were granted the rare favour of being invited within the Forbidden City so that they might themselves set up the apparatus of these gifts, and were even regaled with dishes sent from the imperial table. Soon after they installed a small observatory so that the emperor, unable as we have seen to leave the neighbourhood of the palace, might himself watch the movements of the heavens. In January 1638 there were eclipses of both the sun and the moon, and he was able to see for himself the superior and striking exactitude of the calculations of the European scientists.

As can be imagined, other mathematicians, including Muslims, were most unhappy at being supplanted in this way. On November 8, 1633 the great Paul Hsü Kuang-ch'i died, to be mourned by every missionary in China, and by many others including the emperor. The loss of this patron gave the Jesuits' 'rivals' an unexpected opportunity. The attack was led by the old and splenetic Wei Kung, who had the advantage moreover of having once been a pupil of Hsü Kuang-ch'i's successor. He was given permission to open a school of astronomy of his own and here he spent his time ferreting out errors made by Schall and Rho. If he had the good fortune to find one, however trifling, then the cry was raised: 'The Fathers are dunces; they are miles from the facts!' Wei Kung succeeded in creating some uneasiness in official circles; but he died before any serious damage was done. An attack from another direction followed. A scholar whose son had studied at the Jesuit astronomical school for two years built no hopes on discrediting Western science, but presented to the Court and to the chief eunuch a 'report' of which the gravest accusation ran: 'These foreigners insult the greatest of our people. Confucius, the Master of our masters, they relegate to hell, and with him our most religious emperors, Yao and Shun.' This time the Court was disturbed. A messenger was dispatched to the Fathers ordering the immediate handing over of those works which dealt with the Christian Law. Experts scrutinized these line by line, but nothing incriminating was to be found. The emperor was now angry in proportion to his previous disquiet. The scholar who had tried to use the imperial court for his own ends was exiled, and his observatory was razed to the ground.

There were other attempts to discredit the new astronomers in favour at Court. One unfortunate man of some scientific learning stood forth and said directly that the Father John Adam had committed many and terrible crimes; it was a well-known, proved fact. The emperor promptly had the man put in chains and half-starved until he admitted that he had been suborned by rival mathematicians. More unfortunate still was another slanderer appropriately named K'o. His accusations were that the Western scientists had brought chaos to the astronomical institute; Schall was not the reformer but the corrupter of the Calendar; the confusion must be set right and the cause of it sent into exile. This man was first sent away and then the emperor commanded the relevant officials to consider a punishment for his insolence. A Muslim who was involved hurried to see K'o and tell him what was happening. He found him in the middle of his meal surrounded by his family; and on learning of his very real, indeed terrifying, danger, K'o turned pale, collapsed and died on the spot.

The emperor had firmly taken the part of the Fathers in all this campaign of disparagement. But Ch'ung-chên was not a man of rock-like character; and almost daily came the loud ac-

cusations, the insidious whispers. It was difficult to believe that
the seed of distrust would not finally take root, and certainly
Schall was never at ease. Then the occasion came and the emperor believed that he had indeed been deceived. An eclipse of
the moon was forecast for October 19, 1641. Ch'ung-chên
commanded the Chinese and Muslim mathematicians to observe
it, making use of the instruments recently installed in the
palace by the Europeans. Afterwards they made their report
(a true one): they found that their observations differed by a
quarter of an hour from the calculated predictions of the Europeans themselves. Ch'ung-chên was filled with consternation.
Here was the truth of the accusations that the Western astronomers were ignorant. And they had duped him! He cried out
in his wrath: 'By our imperial will, the correction of the Calendar is not to be attempted again; in spite of everything, the
ancient one is the less imperfect.' By good fortune, however,
this was one of the not infrequent occasions when an imperial
edict lost its way in the bureaucratic maze; the Board
of Rites held it up and it became one of a mass of abortive decrees.

Schall in the meantime was kept informed of the game being
played out in the palace; and he knew the cause of the astronomical divergence. The emperor had ordered that certain idols[1]
which he had previously caused to be removed should be returned to their places. The astronomical instruments were in
the way and had to be dismantled, and the palace eunuchs,
whether through ignorance or intentional carelessness, had set
them up again in an unsuitable place. By dint of pressing en-

---

[1] It must be remembered that the complexities of Chinese thought and
religion ranged through the high-minded charm of Confucian ethics and
ancestor worship, the mystical or semi-mystical austerities of pure Buddhism
and its popular manifestations in the full panoply of temples, 'idols', relics,
and so on, various forms of Taoism, to most primitive superstitions in which
localized spirits, malevolent or not, played (and no doubt still play) a great
part.

treaty, Schall obtained the favour of entry into the palace in order to place the apparatus in a better position. He had the emperor informed of the reason for all this, announcing also an eclipse of the moon on November 3. When the time came the emperor, surrounded by eunuchs but having excluded the mathematicians, set himself to watch. He had the satisfaction of observing the complete accord between the phenomenon presented to his eyes and Schall's calculations. Ready as ever to issue new decrees, he published a fresh edict in which he commanded the immediate adoption of the methods of the European astronomers. There were attempts to make this a dead letter; but the enemy's sting was drawn.

Schall, however, was experiencing opposition not only from those who lived around him but from the other side of the world. The Chinese astronomers had some unlikely allies: Roman theologians. They were concerned about this Chinese Calendar of which they now began to hear so much. It seemed to them that the Chinese Era was irreconcilable with the demands of the Roman Martyrology and with various ecclesiastical writings; thus it would be wrong for missionaries to lend themselves to work on the Calendar. To put things in perspective, and aware of the ignorance of those who were so hasty in their condemnations, Schall wrote a dissertation on the Chinese Era, drawing attention to its existence simply as a method of computing time. This he sent in September 1634 to the vice-provincial in China, who was now Father Furtado. Following the reception of this, a local commission of theologians was set up and, after lengthy discussions of Schall's arguments, it decided on December 20, 1637, that Chinese chronology as it was set forth by Schall could certainly be accepted. With this encouragement Father Furtado had the idea of the foundation of a European astronomical bureau similar to the one under the direction of Muslim astronomers; but Schall knew this was proceeding too fast. 'It would irritate Chinese pride quite unnecessarily, and provoke hatred and even worse jealousy than before,' is what he said, and his counsel was followed.

Schall's position as premier mathematician and astronomer was confirmed. The emperor esteemed him most highly, convinced that he was a man of boundless knowledge.

In July 1642, Chiu, the minister of war, honoured Schall with a visit. There was the customary exchange of compliments, the polite conversation. Gradually, as if by chance, it turned in the direction of the technique of artillery. Chiu was sure that the construction of cannon had no secrets for such a learned man, and without further ado presented Schall with an imperial edict commanding that he should manufacture them! The background to this action may be found in the growing revolts and rebellion in parts of the empire; as we shall see, these were in due course to lead to great changes. The startled priest protested the peaceful nature of his mission and stressed his practical inexperience of such work, without noticeable effect on the war minister who, as he said, was charged simply with carrying out the emperor's commands. Schall's pleas were carried to Ch'ung-chên but he would have none of them. Men and materials were provided, and Schall had perforce to set to work. In his new role of engineer he did not neglect Christian apostleship. He had indeed, first and foremost, to think of a way of forestalling the worship which the workmen would pay to the spirits of the fire in his foundry. In its place, he offered a Christian rite. He set up close by a statue of Christ and, wearing surplice and stole and with his head covered according to Chinese custom, he invited all around him to join in calling on the living God.

There was, of course, jealousy once again and many stratagems were devised to wreck Schall's work. All the same, twenty sizeable cannon were soon completed. The emperor was enraptured at the sight of these fine pieces of ordnance and their easy handling. He gave an order for five hundred, of not more than sixty pounds in weight so that the troops might bring them back with them if they had to retreat. Schall knew his soldiery. He smiled at the thought of Chinese men at arms solemnly refusing to jettison any encumbrance, and these were hardly slight, as they took to their heels; but he went back to work.

While he was still engaged on this job, the emperor requested his views on military strategy. As soon as possible, he was to submit a plan for the defence of the capital. Within a few days Schall had conveyed to him a wooden model showing what he saw as the essential fortifications, laying emphasis on triangular bastions. This was approved and the work put in hand; but the eunuchs intervened with some success this time and another plan, that of one of the emperor's councillors, was put into practice. As he passed one of the revised, square bastions, Schall remarked wryly that if he were the enemy it would be through this position that he would gain possession of the city.

It may seem odd for a missionary to be involved in such war-like enterprises. In spite of his active aid in the defence of Macao, Schall certainly thought so. His feelings had been made clear to the emperor, but this having no effect, he carried out what was commanded with a good grace; the work itself de-manded the exercise of his undoubted talents, and it gave him a certain satisfaction to do it well. It brought no condemnation or criticism in his time, and he must have had the approval or, at least, the permission of his superiors. The kind of issues in-volved have already been touched on. The Catholic Church recognizes and, according to the occasion, justifies the human impulse to take up arms; she does not even require that her priests should refuse to co-operate in the wholesale conscription of certain modern Continental countries, though she is not very happy about it. The particular things which weighed here with Schall were these. In the first place the missionaries were genuinely attempting to become Chinese citizens, and therefore

Schall saw it not as some missionary 'ploy' but as a moral duty
to obey the lawful (or 'just' in the theological sense) commands
of the sovereign. Secondly, and very importantly for Schall, his
cannon were for use in the defence of a civilization which was
in many respects equal to those of Greece and Rome. Its laws,
ethics, philosophy and literature were lofty, rich and profound;
it was a dazzling prospect to conceive of a time when they should
be pervaded, activated and purified by the leaven of the Gospel.
The enemy were not only local rebels but also the Manchus,
always a threat on the northern border, barbarians to the
Chinese, persecutors most likely, and certainly an unknown
quantity; Schall saw them very much as Jerome did the Huns
overflowing into the Roman Empire twelve hundred years before. The consequences of refusing to aid the emperor might be
terrible. The Calvinist Dutch, too, were always on the watch for
the opportunity of getting a foothold in China and once that had
happened it might be impossible ever to retrieve the situation.
The famous battle at Macao would have been in vain! From the
practical view-point it would have been clearly mistaken, even
dangerous, not to accede to what the emperor saw as a perfectly
normal request. To offend him, to lay themselves open to all
the attacks of the jealous eunuchs and officials waiting for just
this moment, was an invitation first to disfavour, then to persecution, then perhaps to exile and the loss of the mission altogether. The doors of China, opened with such patience, work
and suffering, might swing to again. Schall made as full use as
possible of the necessity. He not only cast cannon and worked
out plans of fortification, but took the opportunity to make
astronomical and optical instruments and even hydraulic
machines (of a kind not common in Europe at the time).

Ch'ung-chên was more generous with praise than with more
solid rewards. Hsü Kuang-ch'i had been a friend with his
purse as in every other way; but after his death there were days
when the imperial astronomers did not have enough to eat. This

was one of the periods when Schall thought with especial affection and reverence of his patron, Adam, who himself had been bound to hard and apparently unrewarding labours, hardships which fortified the body and tempered the soul. Then, on April 27, 1638, Giacomo Rho, Schall's friend and associate, died after a very short illness, despite the ministrations of the best doctors in Peking. Many officials took part in the great funeral procession and the emperor, who was represented, appears suddenly to have woken up. He thereupon gave the Jesuit Fathers the considerable sum of 2,000 *taels* and Schall was personally granted a salary of twelve *taels* a month.

This was soon followed by a signal honour: the presentation of an imperial *pai-pien*—four Chinese characters chosen by the emperor, embroidered on a silk scroll and surrounded by the coils of the Chinese dragon. The emperor had no higher mark of favour to confer. The characters he selected read: *Ch'in— pao—t'ien—hsüeh*, 'The emperor praises and commends the celestial doctrine'. Celestial doctrine was, possibly consciously in Chinese fashion, ambiguous. The Jesuits had used it in their books to signify Christianity; and while it could in public be tactfully taken to refer to astronomy, it gave them room to welcome the *pai-pien* as a compliment to their religion. The imperial scroll was brought to their residence on January 6, 1639, the procession winding its way through the streets of Peking headed by four heralds to warn the populace to make the Chinese prostration, the *k'o-t'ou*. With the *k'o-t'ou* again it was received by Schall and Longobardo, their students, and officials involved in the Calendar. Public interest was enormous; crowds surrounded the house while a banquet was held within.

The imperial *pai-pien* was followed, no doubt in imitation, by two from great dignitaries. One from the head of the councillors (the chief *Kolao*) was a testimonial to the Jesuits and their religion; the other was from the president of the Board of Rites, likening the work of the astronomers Schall and Rho to that of two famous learned men of tradition, Hsi and Ho. Jesuit houses in the empire received copies of the imperial *pai-pien* which were displayed in order that the local officials might come and pay their respects. The Imperial Gazette (it is to be remembered that the Chinese had known of printing and paper for many centuries) also published widely all the news about the Calendar and the favours granted by the emperor to the European scientists.

Much of this was, of course, by way of a triumph for Adam Schall, and a profound encouragement in the midst of so much slow toil and patient looking-ahead. There seemed to be a movement of life and change going through the vast Chinese organism; a kind of new birth, signalized of course most plainly in the fast growing numbers who regarded the missionaries with respect and then interest, finally themselves being born again in baptism.

Father Schall now turned his mind to carrying this consequence of the respect won for their scientific achievements into the very heart of the palace. If he was to draw the imperial prisoner towards the freedom of Christ he was going to need far greater strategy than even he had used hitherto.

In 1640, the spinet which Matthew Ricci had presented to Ch'ung-chên's grandfather, Wan-li, was found among the imperial treasures, and the emperor expressed a desire to hear it played. It need hardly be said that it was Father Schall who was to put it in order. With the help of a Brother, Christopher Hsü Fu-yuan, he carried out the repairs. He also composed a method for the playing of the spinet, providing as one of the set pieces a psalm translated into Chinese with a plainsong accompaniment.

Schall took this opportunity to present two further gifts to the emperor. When Father Trigault returned from his famous excursion to Europe, some twenty years ago now, he had brought

I : The Imperial Palace in Peking in the time of Matthew Ricci, about 1610.

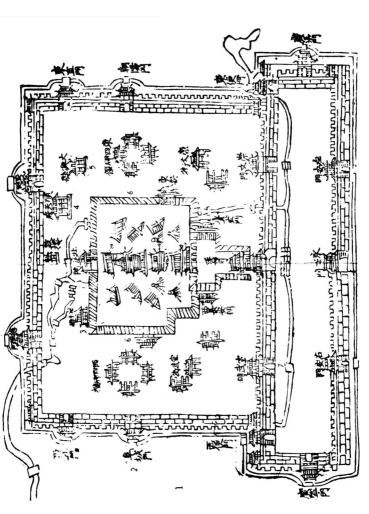

II. Plan of the City of Peking, from the *Annals of Peking*, 1593. 1. Cemetery of Sciala. 2. Feuccemi Gate. 3. Palace of the Sub-Prefect of Yuanping. 4. Palace of the Governor of Peking. 5. Palace of the Sub-Prefect of Tahsing. 6. Enclosure of the Imperial Palace. 7. Süenu Gate: Ricci's house was supposed to be near here.

with him presents to the emperor from the Duke of Bavaria which, for the usual complex reasons of protocol, had never reached their destination. Two of these now accompanied the presentation of the spinet. The first was a manuscript life of Christ; a hundred and fifty pages of parchment containing beautiful illustrations of the principal events, each one matched with the Gospel account. Schall added to this a Chinese translation engraved in gold lettering on the back of the pictures, with also a fuller résumé of the whole Gospel. The four evangelists were portrayed on the silver covers. The second gift was a charming representation of the adoration of the Magi finely worked in coloured wax.

These things were presented to the emperor on September 8, 1640. We know from an account that reached Schall later that when they were brought into the emperor's presence his behaviour was quite different from the usual distant smile or casual glance with which gifts were received. He examined them with real interest and care. The manuscript he took up and was soon lost in it. Then the chief empress was called and, pointing to the wax image of the child Jesus, Ch'ung-chên said: 'He is greater than all our most revered holy men,' whereupon the empress bowed to the ground in the k'o-t'ou. The two gifts were then placed in the palace throne room where the emperor's consorts and vast entourage were told to come and pay their respects to the 'great King'. For ten days they filed past; then the precious objects were removed to his treasure house, but not to be forgotten like so many other presents. Often the emperor would contemplate the wax sculpture and read over and over the story of the life of the King of kings. He was heard to lament as he took his walks: 'Who will expound all this to me?' But he was still living in a prison.

It was a prison, however, which was already gradually being penetrated. Schall himself was allowed inside it only on the rarest occasions, and never of course could he come face to face with Ch'ung-chên. But there was a world of people who lived within, whose very existence revolved around the emperor. There were Christians among the palace eunuchs; two for instance, Achilles (P'ang T'ien-shou) and Nereus, had been baptized as early as 1632. More valuable still was Wang, who became a Christian in 1635, taking the name Joseph. Schall had recognized the potential qualities in the pride and vigour of this eunuch of high position, and now he was a Christian it was through him that Schall was able to reach the palace ladies.

To understand the significance of this we must remind ourselves of the constitution of the imperial household. Only eunuchs and women were allowed to come into direct contact with the emperor. This meant that not only were there very great numbers of women, consorts, concubines, ladies-in-waiting, but many of them were highly educated and performed semi-official tasks as skilled and trusted secretaries, sometimes writing out, for example, drafts of imperial edicts.

Wang, then, in close consultation with Father Schall, set about making the 'celestial doctrine' known among the ladies. His first convert took the name Catherine. Then he raised his eyes higher. The women, like the eunuchs, formed a kind of hierarchy and there were twelve of highest rank; they were very close to the imperial throne. By 1637 three of these were Christians, with the names Agatha, Helen and Isabella (Elizabeth); Agatha in particular was esteemed by the emperor for her virtue and intelligence. In the same year, thirteen conversions are mentioned among ladies of other ranks or classes, and there were also Antonia and a second Agatha (who had been nurse to the previous emperor) who were of the first class but were retired. By 1638 the number of Christian ladies had risen to twenty-one, in 1639 to forty and in 1642 to fifty.

These ladies developed a kind of Christian community within the walls of the palace, a rather restricted community necessarily, which had some characteristics of a religious order.

There was mutual criticism, and even punishment, offered and accepted for 'disobedience' to Wang or unkindness to their non-Christian fellows. The empress was much impressed that anyone should inflict blows on herself in penance for harsh words flung at another in a moment of temper. In a chapel dedicated to our Lady, Wang frequently gathered them together for prayer, and gave them instruction which he in turn received by letter from Schall. The Fathers sent them rosaries and relics, too, and the blessed images of the Lamb of God, the *Agnus Dei*, which played such a part in the piety of the time.[1] The circumstances requiring it, Wang himself administered the sacrament of baptism to new converts in the chapel.

In their far from easy situation the ladies were given the classic counsel: use judgment and discretion, but eschew clear betrayal of your religion for the sake or fear of public opinion. Someone much favoured by the emperor, like Agatha, could find herself in a position of real danger, especially when her duties involved accompanying him to the temple. She stood quietly aside while he knelt and offered sacrifice. They worked busily to give what aid they could to the Christian fathers and to spread their teaching in the palace. They collected alms and made adornments for churches. In their work among their companions in the palace, a very young girl, Secunda, is remembered especially for her part in bringing no less than seven ladies to Christianity.

The unusual qualities of these ladies and the character of their way of life were recognized by Father Furtado when, in 1640, he appointed one of them superior or directress of the community. It was all the more remarkable when we realize that they could not ever hear Mass. Father Schall was sometimes able to say Mass for the Christian eunuchs when he penetrated

[1] They were, for instance, among the objects expressly forbidden to be brought into England in the time of Queen Elizabeth I; see accounts of the arrest and trial of Bd. Cuthbert Mayne.

into the palace, but to have gone near the palace ladies in their chapel or anywhere else would have been inconceivable—and calamitous—in the Chinese view of things. Cut off from the sacraments, these ladies experienced the discovery of God's living presence made, and taught to their ancient forefathers in the spirit, by Jeremias when he was deprived of his beloved Temple worship: 'I will implant my law in their innermost thoughts, engrave it in their hearts' (Jer. 31 : 33).

There is no doubt that Ch'ung-chên and his chief empress were impressed. When, for instance, one of the non-Christian ladies picked a quarrel with a Christian and informed the empress, capping the complaint with the accusation that the woman had been baptized, the empress was unmoved and indeed declared that Christian doctrine was most excellent while all others had strayed from the truth. The emperor took certain steps which might have been thought significant. He avoided converse with his own Buddhist priests (bonzes); idols were removed from his suite; the ladies, even the courtesans and the empresses, were encouraged to become Christians. But he was, to use the old phrase, as weak as water; the bonzes and the idols (as has already been mentioned) both came back into favour. Schall, however, knew the emperor's unrest of spirit and the essential goodness of his heart, and he retained his hopes. They were to be most rudely shattered when enemies rose up against the emperor not only in the empire but within the capital and the court, and Ch'ung-chên's instability erupted into hysteria and suicide. To his dying day Adam Schall maintained, together with his devout prayers for the emperor's final salvation, the conviction that he would have become a Christian had he been granted time.

Schall was still at work in the rest of the city and beyond. He continued his normal pastoral care as a priest in Peking; and in 1637 we hear of him in Hokien a hundred miles away

preaching and baptizing fifty catechumens. He was away when
Father Rho died, and Father Longobardo awaited his return
for those unforgettable funeral rites, the public procession
with its lights and swinging censers, the singing of the solemn
Mass of Requiem.

Schall devoted a great deal of his time to the learned men who
frequently visited him, drawn by his fame as mathematician
and astronomer. Learning and official position were interwoven
in Chinese life, and the system of examinations was complex
and extremely exacting. The influence of the mandarin, both
directly and indirectly, was therefore enormous. The great
Christian mandarin Paul Hsü Kuang-ch'i, whose name runs
like a golden thread through these times, though himself of
the older generation, venerated Schall as a father. He bought a
house for himself and his family near the Jesuit residence so
that he could hear Mass without obstacle, refusing in church
to accept that reserved place with which Western as well as
Chinese custom would flatter the socially distinguished. His
learning and breadth of mind, essential simplicity and love of
God remind us forcibly of his Italian contemporary, Robert
Bellarmine, and in fact across the wastes of sea and land they
knew something of each other. Another of Father Trigault's
gifts brought back from his journey to Europe had been a letter
of greeting from the Church in the West to the Christians of
China written by Cardinal Bellarmine. It was Hsü Kuang-ch'i
who was given the much-coveted task of replying to him on behalf of the Chinese, especially of course the Christian mandarins. When he came to die, Adam Schall was beside his bed
in that house where it was hard to find money for medicines
because of the constant alms-giving to all in need.

Schall had little time and, it appears, little inclination for
apostleship by the pen, which would have seemed to be an
obvious method among the highly literate Chinese. Inevitably,

he did a certain amount of writing. As well as his small work
produced at Sianfu, he composed a two volume work on Divine
Providence (1629), a discourse on the Beatitudes (1634), and
a Life of Christ (1640) which was followed in three years time
by a more extended study of the origins of Christianity. These
writings were well received and played their part in his mission;
but it is not on them that his reputation chiefly rests.

Looking around them in the year 1643, the Jesuit missionaries
were able to see a great deal to give them satisfaction and encouragement, much of it due to the brilliant labours of Father
Schall. The name of Christian was no longer one of social embarrassment or dishonour. The emperor himself was known to
hold the Christians and their teachings in especial respect, and
this of course had its effects throughout the empire. Local
officials now looked on them with a favourable eye, and conversions grew apace. The missionaries themselves were still
pitifully few in number: in about 1640 they consisted of
twenty-four priests and three brothers; but the number of
baptisms, including those of the children of newly converted
parents, increased the Christian population yearly: by 2870 in
1634, 5480 in 1639, 5400 in 1641, 4824 in 1643. Christians
were making themselves felt in public life, even in the army:
a general who had taken the Christian name of Luke had the
cross of Christ painted on his ensigns, and his nephew too,
Ignatius, placed his flotilla of five hundred junks under the
standard of the crucified Lord.

While Father Rho is not to be forgotten, it is the vice-provincial's words about Schall which may be quoted here. Father
Furtado was writing to the general of the Order, Father
Vitelleschi, and he expressed the widespread admiration for and
appreciation of Adam Schall's achievements. His writings, the
life of Christ presented to the emperor himself, the apostleship
of the palace ladies, these are mentioned, and then Furtado
sums it up: 'Our work has been made possible by his dedicated

labours.' The vice-provincial concludes with the hope that the general will send Father Schall an expression of his pleasure and approbation.

The date of this letter was February 2, 1641, the feast of the presentation of the child Jesus in the Temple, when the people in the churches hold candles in their hands and the words of Simeon are sung again and again: *Lumen ad revelationem gentium, et gloriam plebis tuae Israel:* 'This is the Light which shall give revelation to the Gentiles, this is the glory of thy people Israel.'

The Coming of the Manchus

W HEN Father Furtado was writing to the general of the
Society of Jesus, the mission was already in danger.
The Ming dynasty, after nearly three centuries of
achievement and glories, was tottering to its end. Ch'ung-chên
was intelligent, well-intentioned and upright; but he had not the
stature to deal with the multitudes of eunuchs and through them
with the corruption which was eating into the administration of
the empire. The emperor was driven to appeal spasmodically
first to the generals and then to the officials. The eunuchs did
not forgive him. They did not attack him directly, but bided
their time; nor did they have long to wait.

The Manchus, often called by the more generic name Tartar,
were always a threat on the northern borders. The Great Wall,
built two hundred years before Christ to keep out the hordes of
barbarian Huns (*Hsiung-nu*) who had not yet turned their
attentions westwards, was still maintained, and to some purpose.
Since Schall had been in China, in 1629, the Manchus had
thrown themselves at the Wall and breached it in three places,
ravaging the countryside and reaching south towards Peking.
The Chinese were conscious of the Europeans' skill in war and

72

their effective armaments, and Hsü Kuang-ch'i had obtained
the emperor's permission to ask the help of the Portuguese at
Macao. After some difficulty, a tiny troop, armed with muskets
and cannon and led by Gonzales Texeira Correa went to the
support of a Chinese army largely disaffected through lack of
pay, which the eunuchs were keeping back. But they had the
decisive effect of driving the Manchu soldiers, who were well
trained but had not before encountered Western firearms, back
from Chochow. Texeira offered to obtain more highly-skilled
Portuguese, but though the offer was accepted it was never put
into practice. The Manchus had in fact withdrawn and the
officials—encouraged by bribes from their own Cantonese merchants who were jealous of growing Portuguese influence—
stated that the help was not needed.

Behind a great deal of this mismanagement was hostility towards Ignatius Sun Yüan-hua, a Christian of great probity,
general of the army and holder of altogether too many high
offices. A considerable number of his own men were in fact
Manchus who were fighting for the Chinese. What with this
and the lack of pay, the time came when they turned against
their masters and, in spite of Sun's valiant efforts to prize their
money out of the eunuchs and to pacify them generally, they
stormed Têngchow. Texeira and other Portuguese were killed
in its defence and Sun was taken prisoner. The rebels did their
best to persuade the general, for whom they had great respect,
to go over with them to the Manchus. He loyally refused, and
his captors very honourably released him and another Christian
on his staff, Michael Chang Tao—and thus delivered them into
the hands of their fellow Chinese. They were court-martialled
and condemned to be beheaded; another Christian who was
involved, the distinguished mandarin Philip Wang Chêng,
escaped with his life. Hsü Kuang Ch'i used all his powers and
influence to save them, but to no avail; their enemies were in too
strong a position, and could call on the convenient doctrine that

the local official was solely responsible for all that happened where he was in charge.

Before they went to execution they had a most unexpected visitor. A coal merchant with blackened face and sack on his shoulders had occasion to enter the prison: it was Adam Schall, come to hear their last confessions and to bring them the Blessed Sacrament. He managed to remain with them for a day and a half before their death, which they met with cheerfulness and serenity. The exact date seems uncertain; it has been given as September 7, 1632.

The local revolt was not successful and the Manchus were temporarily held in check. In 1636, however, there was a new and sinister sign. The Manchu ruler publicly adopted the Chinese mode of royal titles: his dynasty was thenceforth to be called Ch'ing ('great and everlasting') and he himself was to be known as Ch'ung-ti. All the same, it seems improbable that the Manchus would have overwhelmed China had it not been that that country was 'a beehive about to swarm'. Rebel leaders were appearing who attracted sometimes thousands of adherents. One of these raised his eyes to the imperial throne itself. Li Tzu-ch'êng made himself master of his own province of Shensi and moved on into Shansi. The towns yielded to him and soldiers from the army sent against him by the emperor went over to his side in such numbers that the responsible minister strangled himself in despair at the disgrace. Li's support was largely won through his intelligent move of handing over the large estates which he won to a peasantry starving through official maladministration.

It was in this crisis that the emperor had turned to Schall, demanding the manufacture and supply of the kind of arms which had so daunted the Manchus at Chochow. But armaments and fortifications were of little use when all was rotten within.

The rebel gave himself an imperial title, declared that Sianfu was to be his capital, and swept on; on April 23, 1644, his army was outside the walls of Peking. The city should have been impregnable. Her excellent ramparts now boasted a good number of new, highly effective cannon. The emperor could call on 70,000 trained men; and these he disastrously placed under the command of 3,000 eunuchs. Li Tzu-ch'êng had paused when he came in sight of Schall's cannon; and while he did so, in the early hours of April 25, the western gate was opened by Ts'ao-ch'un, the eunuch who was there in command. As the insurgents poured in, the emperor took to horse with a number of still faithful followers and made for the south gate of the city. Here, however, the eunuchs who one would have supposed might well have let him go, trained Schall's cannon on him, and he turned and rode to the east gate. In doing so, he passed by the Jesuit residence and Schall, with what thoughts and feelings at his first and last sight of Ch'ung-chên can be imagined, watched his headlong flight. Once again the guns were trained on the emperor and, like a hunted animal, he again turned back on his tracks and returned to the palace.

Here he came upon his chief consort, his three sons and his daughter. The empress he told to hang herself, and the sons to go into hiding where best they could. His daughter was only fifteen, and the distracted father tried to slay her with his own hands rather than allow her to fall into the grasp of the soldiers. The terrified young girl warded off the blow from her father's sword, which slipped sideways and cut off her hand. She fled, leaving a trail of blood on the palace floor as she went. Like a madman, Ch'ung-chên ran from the palace once more and climbed a little hill just to the north, known as Mei shan, Coal Hill. Here he slashed his left arm and with a Chinese writing brush left a last message to Li Tzu-ch'êng painted in blood on the skirt of his garment: 'To the new emperor, Li. Do not oppress my people; do not employ my ministers.' Heartfelt words and not ungenerous, as Schall remarks. Then he took off his shoes, threw away his imperial head-dress and hanged himself from a rafter in a summer-house. It was not until a month later that the Manchus discovered his body which they buried with all due honours among his forebears of the Ming dynasty. His is the last of the thirteen great Ming Tombs (all but three of the Ming dynasty) which today are still the object of excursions from Peking.

Adam Schall in his invaluable *Memoirs*[1] wrote the emperor's epitaph: 'This was the lamentable end of perhaps the greatest and most powerful monarch on earth. He was only thirty-six years old, and was inferior to none in ability and qualities. He died abandoned by all, the victim of the betrayal of his servants and officials but also of his own mismanagement. With him the dynasty which bore the name Ta-ming, the Brilliant Realm, came to an end after 276 years, and their kindred who numbered 80,000 died out also. He did not renounce the religion of his ancestors, but he rendered great service to the Church of Jesus Christ; Catholicism had already gained a number of adherents in the time of his grandfather, but he did not merely tolerate it, he extolled and encouraged it for the greater good of his people. More still would he have done if the tragic course of history had not so suddenly brought him to his end.' Patent in this is Schall's own generous and ever-hopeful spirit.

Li Tzu-ch'êng entered the capital that day with 300,000 men. The pillage began. Houses were sacked, the people in the streets knocked down and robbed. Schall was in charge of the Christian community, and made it his especial care to watch over the safety of the women. In the Jesuit residence people gathered in the chapel to pray; and when their new masters came to the door only an old carpet was carried off, and that with permission. Someone, no one knows who or why, placed

---

[1] Published in various editions, though unfortunately to some extent 'edited'; e.g. *Historica Relatio de ortu et progressu Fidei Orthodoxae in Regno Chinensi*, Ratisbon, 1672. A manuscript is in existence to which Father Duhr made reference when he prepared his version of this *Life*.

a notice on the wall of the house warning soldiers to respect the 'European Father'.

A few days later, two Chinese officials came to call and accompany Schall to the palace. This seemed dangerously polite, and he exclaimed characteristically: 'Where are the chains? Here are my neck and my hands for them.' A third official arrived on the scene and tried in vain to appease him; it was much to his surprise therefore when he was given a warm welcome at the palace and was assured of protection and security. More startling still, the new man in power rose to his feet, sent away the women who were entertaining him, and taking Schall by the hand, called for Chinese tea. He gave orders, too, for a meal to be served at which Schall was to sit at his side, but this Schall politely declined; he wanted to get back to his charge before nightfall. He was seen home with every mark of respect. It seemed as if Schall and his flock would now be safe from annoyance, but he was taking nothing for granted. He visited the Christians constantly, bringing them the steadying influence of his presence, the repeated exhortation to prayer and hope in God, the encouragement of his own prayers. There were hours and days of sudden peril and fear. A Christian who owned a large house had given refuge to forty-four people including a number of young girls. Some roaming soldiery tried to force their way in, but were met at the doorway by two young men, terrible in demeanour and brandishing great clubs. The soldiers took to their heels.

Li, however, was master of the capital city; he was not master of China. He knew this, and was distinctly evasive when the astronomers hurried round to present him with the Calendar for the following year that he might choose the day for his coronation. It was necessary, risky though it might seem, to subdue the imperial army which was on the frontier guarding it against the Manchus. For this purpose Li put 200,000 men in the field, leaving a garrison of 3,000 in Peking.

Wu San-kuei, general of the imperial forces, had delayed marching to the help of the emperor in Peking (though not, certainly, for reasons of disloyalty), and he was now ensconced at Shanhaikuan at the east end of the Great Wall. Li was wise enough to see the danger of engaging an army in battle at that time and place, and he attempted to force the general into co-operation by bargaining with the life of his father who was in Li's hands. He is said to have brought the old man before the walls of Shanhaikuan and announced his terms, while the general stood and listened on the rampart. Apart from common human feeling, Chinese filial devotion is a great thing, but loyalty to an emperor, albeit a dead emperor, won. The general fell on his knees begging his father's forgiveness, but his words to Li were: 'My duty is to the emperor and to my country first, and after that, only, to my father. Life indeed is a good gift; but it would be to my eternal shame if I agreed to ally myself with an accursed enemy to the destruction of our land.' The heroic father approved this speech and was carried off to an agonizing death; and to the motive of loyalty in his son's mind was now added that of revenge. (This is Schall's account; there was also a Chinese version which said that Wu San-kuei would have given into the threat—until he heard that Li had appropriated his favourite concubine!)

Wu San-kuei wished to make sure of scattering the rebels to the winds. He looked round for allies, and inevitably his eye fell on the Manchus. An alliance was agreed upon; in return for their aid, the Manchus were to retain a strip of land some hundred miles long which they were already infesting, and were to have freedom of trade with the Chinese empire. The Tartar warriors marched towards Shanhaikuan. First of all their horse-men drove off the undisciplined rebel bands; then the foot-soldiers fell on the men besieging the city. After that, with the help of the troops of Wu San-kuei, it was flight and massacre. Li Tzu-ch'êng sought momentary refuge in Peking, where he took what hardly seems a good opportunity and was crowned, and then fled south again. The Manchu generals pursued, cutting down his soldiers as they went.

Peking was in flames. Li had thoughtfully left its garrison behind with orders to destroy as much of the city as possible. The imperial palace was blazing; the beautifully constructed city gates, the great houses and the homes of the people, all were set on fire. Gun-powder added its explosions. Schall could hear the crashes as the imperial palace fell in, while friends and acquaintances begged him to escape from the city at once, afraid for his life, even more than their own, as a foreigner and friend of the dead emperor. Some of them added the argument that Peking would be no more than a heap of cinders and he himself a prisoner in the hands of the barbarian Tartars; much better for him to go and establish a Christian centre in another place. But his first concern was the Christian community in Peking.

He had, if possible, to take care of the Jesuit residence itself, with its chapel and precious books and even the engraved plates which had been prepared for printing, not to speak of those people who had taken refuge there. Schall behaved with a wholly typical combination of confidence in God and exercise of the powers of his own personality. He tells of three ruffians who followed one of the servants as he came back into the house; they were calmly shown the door and as quietly went away. Almost at once others appeared at the back, having broken through the wall. They came face to face with Schall: 'What's all this?' said he in his most impressive voice. 'Soldiers? You should be ashamed of yourselves, behaving like bandits!' The intruders hung their heads and went off in silence the way they had come. Three days later there was something very like an assault on the house. Two Chinese (who had been nursing a grudge against Schall) led a variously armed crowd against the gate of the compound. Schall knew the Chinese: 'Good at a charge, but with no staying-power,' as were Prince Rupert's cavalry in the English civil war. He seized a great Japanese sabre and presented himself at the gate. At this sight, the mob hesitated, seemed abashed; they began to make excuses: they were looking for plunderers. Then they melted away. Schall comments, not without some pride, that the appearance of his—very luxuriant—beard had its effect in this drama. Schall's role has since been played down, owing no doubt to a certain swashbuckling note in the priest's behaviour. But we have no reason to doubt his account, not least because its spirit and dash and its humour are so typical of the man.[1]

Fire was their second enemy, and one just as terrible. The buildings around were burning and it seemed that the Jesuit residence would catch alight at any moment. It was difficult to know what to do; and again typically he not only and naturally prayed but threw where he could on the roofs blessed *Agnus Dei*. It was noticed that this particular house was not on fire and it now became the centre of the incendiaries' attack. Firebrands were thrown in, the more dangerously in that the wooden roof beams were very dry and there were logs and coal heaped in the compound. However, they were either put out or went out of their own accord. Bundles of dry twigs were now

---

[1] Here is Adam Schall's own vigorous and vivid account of the assault on the Jesuit residence, taken from his *Memoirs*: (seldom has Latin appeared less a 'dead language'):

On the third day the inhabitants of the city formed a body, surrounded the house and made as if to attack it. They set about the outer door with crowbars and when this was broken down they started on the inner door; others meanwhile clambered on to the roof; armed with bars and clubs just as chance had served them in their haste, they tried to break their way in. Admittedly I knew that the Chinese are of cowardly disposition but at that moment I could not guess how far their rage would take them nor what could be the cause of such unaccustomed excitement, so I seized a Japanese sabre and stood in front of the hall by the inner door ready to sustain and repel any attack. Some prayer was answered, for those who had climbed the roof on seeing me thus armed and ready for action and, as it happened, with a beard as long as all theirs, straightway excused themselves and cried that they were looking for robbers but that since there were none inside the house they would immediately go back. When the others heard this they all left.

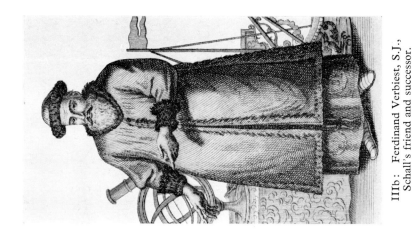

IIIb: Ferdinand Verbiest, S.J.,
Schall's friend and successor.

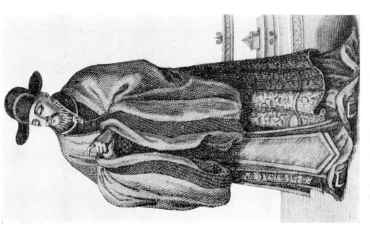

IIIa: Paul Hsü, one of the first
Christian mandarins.

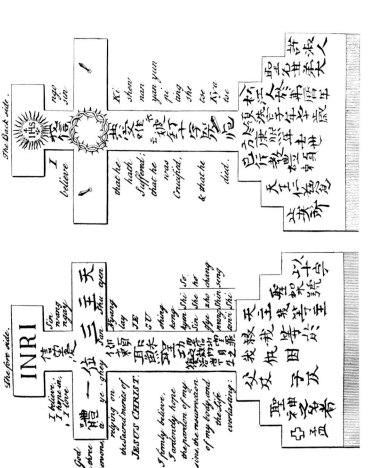

IV. This is the sort of Cross which was used by the Christian Chinese, and frequently buried with them. (The notation and translation was added by the editor of the 1741 volume from which this is taken).

brought, stacked in the gateway and fired. As the praying but otherwise helpless Schall watched, a sudden gust of wind seized the burning brands and scattered them so that they fell for the most part on a nearby temple which was already in ruins. Schall comments that God himself was preparing the place for a new church.

He was most of all struck by what happened in a house adjoining the Jesuit residence in which three rooms had been hired. Here it was that his scientific equipment was kept; books of mathematics, the preparations for printing, and his own works. He had so far made use of only two of the rooms, and their walls were hung with wooden tablets inscribed in the Chinese manner. Schall mourned the loss of so much valuable work when he saw the third room already in flames. Then to his astonishment he realized that the fire was not spreading. In his own words: 'One might have said that an unseen power divided this room from the other two. Not a character was damaged on the wooden tablets, dry and exposed to the heat as they were; the fire appeared to respect the official Calendar.' It was for him a tangible sign of divine blessing on his 'apostleship of science'.

Above all, his care was for the wounded and the distressed, not neglecting even then his responsibilities as a Christian pastor. One man, a Christian of long standing but in secret for fear of the Chinese, came to Schall with an arm in tatters from a small cannon ball. While he gently washed, dressed and bandaged the wounds, Schall spoke to him of the cowardice he had yielded to and the physical suffering which he must now bear the more bravely. The man recovered finally from his rather shocking injuries, as did another of Schall's patients who had had an arrow through his neck. There were others more difficult to save: those whose terror and despair were driving them to suicide. Something impelled Schall one day to visit a nearby house which had so far escaped the fire. He penetrated into an inner room where he was met with the sight of seven people, men and women, hanging from the beams. But two were still alive. He cut them down, worked on them until they regained consciousness and gradually nursed them back to complete recovery.

The chief Manchu general, Dorgon by name, the uncle of the six year old new Manchu king, Fu-lin, now gathered his victorious army and returned to camp round the walls of the capital. He waited for four days, percipient enough to guess the easiest and best way of entering. He was right. Sickened with bloody anarchy, Mandarins and other classes alike came out and begged him to take possession of the city and the imperial palace. All had one desire: order and peace. Dorgon appeared to hesitate. He asked whether all were in agreement that the Tartars should henceforward reign over them. The reply came in the form of words with which welcome is given to the emperor of the Chinese: 'Wan-sui, wan-sui, wan-wan sui!' 'May the emperor reign for ten thousand years, for ten thousand years, for ten thousand times ten thousand years!' The general graciously acceded to so pressing an invitation, and on June 7 he entered the city. On June 8, the Chinese knew that they had indeed acquired a master: the order was given that the North City should be evacuated within three days for the use of the Tartars. This of course meant the abandoning of many official and great residences; and among them was that of the Jesuit fathers.

Schall did not hesitate. He at once addressed a petition to the government saying that he was a European who had lived in Peking for many years, having come to make the Heavenly Law known to all. He possessed, he went on, a church, books and a whole establishment necessary for his work. The late emperor had officially entrusted him with the correction of the astronomical calculations and the reformation of the Calendar, and in his house were a mass of mathematical workings setting out his science; all these might be destroyed, to the great loss of the state, if he had to leave the city. A stranger himself, he made supplication to those who likewise had come from afar to be good enough to permit him to remain in his position.

Taking with him this skilfully worded document, with its appeal both to indulgence and pride, Schall dressed himself in the ordinary garments of the Chinese and went to join the crowd of those petitioning their new rulers. There they waited on their knees, while the suppliants were thinned out quite simply with canes and whips. Schall was not molested, and in due course Fan, a Chinese official who had long supported the Manchus, called him and required his petition. Having glanced over it, Fan put the first question.

'What is meant by this word "church"?'

'It is a place where God, the creator of all things, is given honour.'

'Why don't you say "temple", like everyone else?'

'In order to distinguish the religion which I preach from those of others.'

'Did you have an official position in the Institute of Astronomy? Were you in receipt of a salary?'

'No. I was not an official mathematician; it was my task to oversee those who were.'

Fan seemed quite pleased with these replies, and he told Schall to rise (he had been on his knees all this time) and to come again next day. He assured him that his house would not be touched in the meantime. Two suitably qualified men were directed to verify Schall's words, and when he returned he was given permission to remain in what was now to be the Tartar City. At the same time he was given a notice to this effect, that he might place it over the gate of the Jesuit residence. Its necessity was apparent when he went back again to find house and compound occupied by far from friendly visitors who told him to get out. It was, however, they who retreated, full of respect, when they were shown the official notice. Other Jesuit possessions, near Father Ricci's burial place, were also protected and a second, even more definite, public notice assured Schall of still greater security. This must have been largely due to the impression Father Schall had made on Fan, who continued his benevolence by sending him thirty pieces of gold every year for his alms and his 'temple'. Many of Fan's family, including one of his daughters, were to become Christians.

Four months later, on October 19, 1644, the little emperor entered the Tartar City by the imperial gate. He was the ninth son of the Manchu ruler, Abahai (he who had taken the imperial title of Ch'ung-ti) who had died two years before, and the child had been elected his successor by the council of Manchu princes. We know him by his reign title, Shun-chih; while, as we have seen, Abahai had named the dynasty Ch'ing. His regents here, as in Manchuria, were Dorgon and another uncle, Jirgalang. Dorgon, in particular, was a man of some political acumen. The new emperor was very much his protégé; it was through Dorgon that the more obvious choice, Abahai's eldest son, had been excluded from the succession.

Peking was proclaimed the capital and residence of the new dynasty on October 30. The Chinese general Wu San-kuei had been left to complete the immediate work when Dorgon had returned to enter the capital, and Li Tzu-ch'êng was killed by local people while fleeing towards the province of Hupeh in 1645. Order and peace were not established all at once. Chang Hsien-chung, a rebel of the type of Li, was guilty of barbarous slaughter before he was killed in an affray in 1647 (of this revolt we shall hear more later). There were also a number of attempts to restore the Ming dynasty, of which the last and most serious was that supported by a number of distinguished Chinese Christians, including the palace eunuch who had been baptized in 1632, Achilles P'ang T'ien-shou. He gave active support to the pretender, Yung-ming, a grandson of the old emperor Wan-li, and succeeded in converting many of his family, including the empress dowager who was given in baptism the fairly obvious name of Helena. This close involvement of Christians in the political arena resulted in some odd circumstances, as when both Helena and P'ang T'ien-shou wrote letters asking for the support of Pope Innocent X and the general of the Jesuits in their cause, as well as for more missionaries. These were taken to Europe by Father Michael Boym, who promptly incurred the displeasure of the general for exceeding his proper role as a member of the Society. This kind of support no doubt mainly accounted for the fact that the cause of Yung-ming, who was proclaimed emperor by his followers in 1646, managed to survive for over ten years, when it finally disintegrated, largely through the death of its most able leaders.

Manchu and Chinese were already acquainted with each other; above all, the newcomers were familiar with the Chinese political system and administration and saw no reason to tamper with it to any degree. Indeed the change which caused the most trouble was, not unnaturally, that which affected the personal lives of every man in the empire. This was the edict that the Chinese were to shave their heads and grow a queue after the Manchu manner (in other words the pigtail, which we have come to think of as traditionally Chinese). Certain portraits show us how Father Schall conformed to this legal, though possibly not lawful, demand. Administrative changes were mostly at high level and consisted mainly in bringing Manchus into the Chinese government already in being. The Council of State, for instance, now consisted of seven Chinese and seven Manchu councillors or *Kolao*. A Grand Council of the Crown was also set up to be responsible for the most serious affairs of state. This was an elaborate organization, including princes, Manchu nobles, members of the Council of State and other distinguished and learned men. But it was, as in the past, still the emperor who had the last word, at least in theory.

Adam Schall was now able to return to his scientific studies. He set himself to the composition of the Calendar for 1645, not knowing whether his services would be called on by the new government, but well aware that the Manchus shared the Chinese reverence for the course of the heavens.

He had not long entered on his task when a messenger came to him requesting that he should present himself before the Council of State. The background to this move was as follows. Other astronomers had hastened to present the newly constituted Council with their Calendar for the coming year. In their anxiety to be first, they had taken a risk: it was not a newly reckoned Calendar at all, but one for a previous year given a new name. They were totally unsuccessful. To the curt question as to what this might be, they replied coolly that it was the ancient Calendar of the nation composed according to the new method. It was pointed out to them that the Calendar was clearly full of errors and, more humiliating still, the Manchus in the Council inquired after the European of whom they had heard, who was drawing up a more correct one. This would be a fitting opening for a new dynasty; the astronomers were instructed to see that he came to them at once. They retired; but they did not get in touch with Schall.

When he did not appear, the Council sent their own messenger, rather to Schall's disquiet who knew nothing of all this and wondered what was in the air. However, he was met at the gate by mathematicians of the Institute of Astronomy who pressed around him obsequiously, some of them 'venturing to give him the counsel' that it would be best to say that his own method was not yet absolutely exact and still stood in need of a certain revision. Schall was brusque: 'Your advice is no use at this stage; I shall know what to say when I know what I am asked.—I can promise you nothing.—In any case I see what you would be at; this sudden desire for an alliance after fifteen years of war does not fill me with much confidence.' When he came before the

Council what in fact he said was: 'The Calendar is well in hand: I shall have completed it for the year to come by the end of this month.'

Thereupon his rivals offered the Council their calculations. This was no light thing to be decided, so the 'competitors' were sent home with instructions to return next day after each had studied the other's work. When the time came Schall was able to point out seven considerable errors made by the Chinese mathematicians, while they could find none in his unless it was the novelty of Schall's methods altogether. Schall, then, was entrusted with the task of drawing up the Calendar for the second year of the reign of the emperor Shun-chih. Within a few weeks he had his draft ready for the approval of the Council; and by August 21 he had it prepared for public use. An imperial edict, two days later, commended its accuracy, only remarking a few slight faults—the Manchu town of Fengyang (modern Mukden) had been wrongly named, and the text was too compressed with too small characters.

This success was followed by another, of which Schall was most reluctant to take advantage. An eclipse of the sun was forecast for September 1 of the same year, 1644. Schall presented his calculations, as did the Chinese and Muslim astronomers. But Schall offered a new and original constituent; he had not only made the calculations for observing the eclipse in the capital but in all the chief towns of the empire. This was received with great pleasure. Two ministers were commanded to join Schall and his pupils to observe the eclipse; and many other court officials joined them at the Board of Rites in order to witness on their knees 'the sun's contest with its terrible adversary'. Schall's pupils explained to the ministers what was happening; one of them was even able, with the help of a telescope, to throw the reflection of the celestial bodies on to a piece of paper and in this way to follow out the phases of the 'duel'. Whereupon one of the enthusiastic ministers seized a brush and wrote: 'We members of the Council of State, present at the eclipse, have been convinced that the Chinese and Muslim mathematicians are ignorant, and that only the Europeans can make truly accurate calculations. It is the pleasure and glory of our dominion to have recognized a science which the old rule tried to stifle for twenty years. May this be remembered for ever! ... May the new method be employed for ten thousand years to come!'

One of the ministers made his official report next day, summing it all up in one comprehensive Chinese term which may be expressed in less complex English as 'quite excellent from every point of view'. It was used again in the imperial edict which followed on September 7. We have also Schall's own, less florid, account of the proceedings, which he wrote four days later. If confirmation were needed, this was provided when reports came in of the observations made in various provinces.

This occasion was decisive. By the emperor's command, the method of the Europeans was henceforth to be the official astronomical system. Schall was to be in charge of all astronomical work, choosing which assistants and how many he wanted. But no rumour of a greater honour leaked through to him, and he was genuinely upset when, at the end of the same year, he was informed without warning that the emperor had appointed him the Director of the Institute of Astronomy. He entreated the emperor to spare him the honour, pleading his unfitness, his wish not to accept official public position, the difficulties of the formalities to be regularly observed and their incompatibility with his calling and his normal duties. The emperor (we may perhaps suppose the voice of the chief regent, Dorgon, speaking through his young nephew) countered by offering to do away with or to modify anything that Schall felt to be impossible or awkward. Schall was still so unhappy about it that he sent his refusal to the emperor not once but seven times. The situation was getting embarrassing; kind friends let Schall know that the emperor was becoming wearied and vexed, Schall's obstinacy might do real harm. Driven up against this wall, he consulted Father Furtado as superior of the mission in the north. Father Furtado did not simply advise, in this instance he put him under obedience: he was to accept the office with its duties and insignia. Thus it was that—after a far from soothing correspondence with his superior—Adam Schall became a public personage, taking rank in the fifth class of imperial officials.

Schall was now in a unique position. He had persuaded the last of the Ming emperors to accept his services, but as a private individual, a learned man inferior in status to the Chinese and Muslim astronomers. His position and influence were proportionately variable. Now, as Director of the Institute of Astronomy, he was as it were the pivot on which the life of China turned. As the man who officially drew up the Calendar, and so in Chinese eyes as the interpreter of the wishes of Heaven, he held the destiny of the Celestial Empire in his hands; he was looked up to as a master by the Son of Heaven himself.

It was a hard blow for the astronomers who had been supplanted. Common pride (and Chinese sensitivity to social rebuff) could not submit to this foreigner; above all they could not tolerate the idea that the law of heaven should be laid down for them by a man of the West. Now more than ever, Schall was the enemy to be destroyed. Wary and cunning after past failures, they hatched a more skilful plot. They began by making use of what should have been unexceptionable witnesses, Schall's own pupils. Two students of astronomy were bought over and went about everywhere saying, 'John Adam, jealous of his own learning, is refusing to teach us the new methods, while at the same time he is always disparaging Chinese science. . . . He is proud and arrogant, and disgustingly avaricious. He sees to it that he gets a lot of gifts on top of his official salary.'

This was fairly serious, and it became a good deal more so

when these relatively humble accusers were joined by no less a person than the president of the Board of Rites. He had not forgiven Schall for refusing him the favour of his support for an incompetent Muslim astronomer. He took his chance of revenge and summoned Schall to appear before a court. His accusation was not simply that of pride or greed, but that Schall had made himself Director of the Institute of Astronomy without having received the title officially: 'the foreigner must be condemned'. Schall was on his knees, bare-headed in the blazing sun. This gave him a terrible headache which, he tells us, lasted three days. But the mounting physical discomfort was nothing to the shock he received when it was announced after a two hours' search that the certificate of appointment was not to be found in the archives. With a silent prayer, he made the request that they would be so good as to examine the records once more. This time the document was discovered and produced.

Hearing of all that had taken place, the emperor ordered that the culprits should appear before his council to ask public pardon for their unworthy conduct; the two pupils of the astronomical institute were removed, their places being taken by Chinese Christians. God himself, says Schall in his simple way, saw to the punishment of the authors of this little play: one of them died of the plague, while the principal accuser was assassinated by some disgruntled peasants in his native Shantung and his son, who had just had a 'doctorate' conferred on him, was exiled beyond the Great Wall.

Adam Schall emerged from this latest trial not only unscathed but with an increased reputation. The highest Manchu personages paid him visits; the chief regent, who bore a certain resemblance to that 'honourable man' Brutus, conversed with him a number of times. Schall was also on good terms with the king of Korea who was then staying in Peking, and rendered him what services he could, including an effort to draw him

towards the knowledge of Christ. The approval of the great
may or may not be a valuable witness; but Schall also won the
warm affection of his subordinates for his goodness of heart,
humility and just dealing.

When he had shown his favour so generously to Father
Schall, the emperor all unknowing had raised up a protector for
himself in a time of sudden danger. Shun-chih had decided to
recognize the real services of his uncle, the chief regent, by
erecting two great marble columns at the gate of the imperial
palace, inscribed with Dorgon's praises for the benefit of
generations to come (we may compare the custom of European
classical times, for instance, Trajan's Column in Rome). As it
happens, Schall played a part in this too; he created an impression by considerably easing the transport of the huge marble
blocks, using a system of pulleys previously unknown to the
Chinese. But this was no longer enough for the regent, who had
tasted the delights of power. Ever-ready sycophants encouraged
him to dream of usurping the supreme title of the Son of Heaven.
His first step was to publish edicts in his own name, giving himself therein such pompous appellations as the Father of the
Emperor, the Father of our Country. A kind of imperial palace
with retinue to match, and imperial robes, proclaimed his ambitions for all the world to see. At the same time the young emperor found himself neglected, derided, even in danger. Then
came the project of a new capital. For this, the regent took
seven million gold pieces from the treasury of the state, levied
new taxes and conscripted workmen. The province of Shensi,
where the people were discontented with the present régime,
was already his in sympathy.

The great men of the country feared the worst: a split in the
imperial family and civil war. They lamented the danger, but did
not dare to cross so powerful a man. But Adam Schall, in his
unique position, came to the decision that astronomy must be
brought to bear on the regent, who of course shared the universal

reverence for the Calendar and the courses of the stars. In a long petition, he set out to persuade the regent that all the indications of the celestial science warned him to abandon the project. The regent's immediate reaction was dictated by his ambitions: 'So this man alone dares to oppose me!' However, a prudent *Kolao* spoke up: 'Do not be provoked. The European is doing his duty; and if you refuse to listen to him he may keep silent in the future to your own great harm.' This gave the regent pause, and he commanded Schall's presence on the following day when he pressed him as to whether he was quite sure about what he had set forth. Schall repeated his prognostications. Fear of fighting against the will of heaven thereupon brought Dorgon to a better frame of mind. He gave up his ambitions and stopped the construction of the new capital. On the day this edict was published seven hundred workmen who had been brought in from outside and herded into the ministry of public works were released and sent home. When they learned that their good fortune was due to the European, they turned aside at the Christian chapel and, in thanksgiving, fell on their knees in the road.

As a public sign of his submission to the emperor, the regent undertook a campaign against the disaffected province, making use of cannon and other armaments provided by Schall. The generals were very appreciative of this aid, and more than one of them, becoming governors of provinces later on, expressed their gratitude by favouring the work of the Jesuits in their district. After order had been re-established, Dorgon went into Mongolia to escort to Peking a wife for the emperor. This was his last service to the throne; he died soon after his return, at the end of the year 1650, probably in a hunting accident.

Adam Schall's great good offices towards the imperial family added yet again to the fame and prestige he enjoyed as astronomer. T'ang Jo-wang, 'the son of Father Matthew Ricci', was now universally known. His name had become the missionaries'

password to success. Father Francis Brancato (who laboured
with notable success for many years at Shanghai, with the invaluable help of Candida Hsü, grand-daughter of Paul Hsü
Kuang-ch'i) wrote to the father general on September 27, 1650:
'With God's blessing, it is the general esteem for Father Adam
which facilitates all we do, on our journeys, in the towns and
our relations with officials.' This is echoed by the younger
Father Dias: 'Whatever the distance, Schall is always able to
come to our aid; for we have only to say that we are his companions and brothers and no one then dares say a word against
us.'

Schall himself took this opportunity to show forth publicly
the splendour of the Catholic Church. He planned a church in
the heart of the northern city, giving on to a busy street near one
of the main gates. Inevitably, no doubt, he was inspired by the
great new churches of Rome: this was to be in what is now
known as baroque style, with three aisles, and crowned by a
dome.

The emperor himself and other great men were generous with
financial support, and the work advanced quickly; it was begun
early in 1650 and by the end of the year was almost complete.
An inscription placed over the central doorway commemorated
the Christian apostolate in China, telling its tale briefly from St
Thomas the apostle's supposed visit, through the verified history of early times and the Middle Ages to Matthew Ricci; it
referred to the science of the Europeans now approved by the
new dynasty, ending with these words: 'This new church,
erected by the gateway Tu-men, has been built in honour of
the true doctrine.' The Chinese took an admiring interest in
this first great Western building to be raised in their country.
A hundred and fifteen feet high, forty-five feet wide and eighty
feet long, it dominated all the buildings around. Above the high
altar, a beneficent figure of Christ, surrounded by angels and
apostles, held the globe in one hand and raised the other in

blessing. A copy of the celebrated image of our Lady of the Snow (in the basilica of St Mary Major in Rome) stood on the Lady altar to the left (the 'Gospel side'); the altar on the right (the 'Epistle side') was dedicated in honour of St Michael and all Angels. Two further altars, placed in the body of the church, were in honour of St Ignatius of Loyola, founder of the Society of Jesus, and of St Francis Xavier, one of the first followers of Ignatius, outstanding missionary and the apostle of the East. Letters of gold on the walls set out the principal teachings of Christianity, including the life of Jesus and that of the blessed Virgin Mary; the Ten Commandments; extracts from the catechism; the Beatitudes; and a list of the principal works of mercy. Father Ferdinand Verbiest, colleague and firm friend of Schall, commented that the church could bear comparison with the best in Rome.

Thus the period of the regency came to its close with a striking Christian proclamation of faith. As it turned out, Schall's work had almost entirely benefited from the change in the régime; in the previous reign he could hardly have dreamed of the position in which he now found himself.

A few months after the death of the chief regent, the young but mature Shun-chih (his age has been variously reckoned as twelve, thirteen or fifteen) took the reins of government into his own hands. He was fully aware of what Adam Schall had already done for him and for the wellbeing of his kingdom, and looked on him with enormous respect mingled with affection.

'Ma-Fa'

SHUN-CHIH reigned for ten years. He was generous but fanciful, intelligent but capricious; while he was sovereign over many millions of subjects he was not really master of himself. Sometimes his perspicacity, understanding and liberality were impressive; at others he seemed quite unbalanced and uncontrolled, utterly impatient of opposition, flinging himself against barriers and setting his heart on all kinds of impossible or extravagant projects. This ungovernable animation and exuberance was to show itself in the end as a kind of wild despair.

Even so, in spite of faults and defects, his extreme youth and early death, Shun-chih has a respected place among the emperors of China. His reign was very much better than might have been expected in the circumstances, and is marked for Christianity as a time of unusual prosperity. The credit for this must go largely to the one man in the empire who truly commanded the young emperor's attention and even obedience, Father Schall.

There was now no question of refusal of access to the emperor. More than that, with Schall Shun-chih appeared to forget that he was emperor of China. Rather, Adam Schall was his *Ma-fa*, a Manchu term signifying 'grandpa', with all the respect as well as affection which once at least was associated with the English word. From the start he went out of his way to express his recognition of his benefactor; he declared at a gathering of the governors and great officials of the country: 'I owe a great debt of gratitude to the European master of the Celestial Law. He predicted that if a member of our dynasty [Dorgon, that is] took to himself the imperial dignity, he would die. As well as that, he daily undertakes numerous works for the wellbeing or renown of the State.'

It was some little time before Schall won the temperamental ruler's full confidence; he had to use all his generosity and warmth of character to dispel certain clouds of mistrust. Finally, however, Schall's constant good humour and obvious dis-interestedness and integrity laid the emperor's doubts to rest and he met him henceforth without reserve. On one occasion he commented on the behaviour which raised Schall above those who habitually surrounded the throne, whether courtesans or councillors. It had been remarked that this foreigner was always in the emperor's favour, while other notables came and went fairly frequently. 'You should remark, rather,' said the em-peror, 'on this foreigner's mode of behaviour. It is always the same: never is there anything changeable or fickle in his feelings or attitude.' Another time, an aged, and therefore the more re-spected, dignitary in presenting a request to the emperor was permitted to follow it up with an audience at which he was loquacious. The emperor interrupted him.

'You can save yourself the trouble. I have an excellent master who teaches me all this and a great deal more.'

'That is very good,' replied the aged official, with some dar-ing, 'but that does not prevent one listening also to the counsel of others.'

'You others,' said Shun-chih, 'are simply self-interested;

what you are after is to keep the emperor in leading-strings. T'ang Jo-wang is not one of you. His petitions are full of such goodness, honesty and disinterestedness that when I read them I am often moved to tears.'

Above all, the emperor admired and wondered at Schall's mastery over himself, body as well as mind and soul. Himself goaded by the lusts of the flesh, he could not get accustomed to the idea of a man so free of bondage to natural instinct that he could always command his body. Indeed, for a long time he was in doubt whether it could be so, and for months he conducted a kind of inquiry into the subject. In the evenings, often very late, two or three young noblemen would appear before Schall, ostensibly to question him on various points, in fact to observe what he was doing. When they returned to the court they had to report to the emperor every detail of what they had seen and heard. They never found anything unwonted, still less suspect; as Schall says, he was using the calm of the night hours either to work or to pray. Shun-chih, after many such visits, was convinced. Later, in an honorary commendation published on April 2, 1653, and on a column set up outside the church on March 15, 1657, the emperor brought to public notice Schall's uprightness, zeal, loyalty and wonderful physical integrity. With such experiences, the young man's confidence in Schall grew, and his relationship with his *Ma-fa* became more and more cordial.

In order that they might converse more often and easily the emperor waived the complex formalities of court etiquette, in particular the elaborate performance of the *k'o-t'ou*, a rare privilege. He conferred on him, moreover, what was in fact a privilege of the imperial family when he permitted Schall to have access to him at any time and place. He always greeted him with pleasure and willingly listened to what he had to say. In any case he liked to see him at least once a month and sometimes on these occasions their conversation would continue far into the night. Then a number of young noblemen would escort Father Schall back to his residence, instructed by the emperor that they were not to go too fast, and to take care not to do anything that might startle the Father's horse in case he should be thrown. One of the emperor's habits was to walk at night in the wooded gardens by the palace, and he would send for Schall so that they might converse in these quiet and serene hours. At other times it was in the royal apartments, in his bedchamber itself, that he would confide his doubts and cares to Schall: 'I am doing this so I can talk with you more freely,' he explained.

More careless of convention still, the emperor paid Schall many visits; in the two years of 1656 and 1657 he went to the Jesuit residence twenty-four times. Then he was most the boy, simple and affectionate towards his *Ma-fa*. Appearing without any announcement and making his way straight to Schall's room, he refused any special chair, sitting down where he felt like it—on the bed, a chair by the work table or a simple bench used by ordinary visitors or pupils. It was the custom that a place or chair on which the emperor had deigned to seat himself should henceforth be dedicated to him, no other person might use it. With this mild superstition in mind, Schall once remarked a little mischievously to his guest: 'There is hardly anywhere in the room where you, sire, have not sat down; what are we others going to sit on from now on?' Shun-chih took him up quickly: 'Now even *Ma-fa* is favouring supersition; do as I do, and sit where you want to.' With an easy courtesy which confounded those who confused dignity with etiquette, he poured out questions. He took an interest in everything to do with his host: his studies, rule of life, worship, apostleship and hopes of conversions. By the *prie-dieu* hung a rosary. 'What is that?' asked the emperor. Schall in his reply called in a child who, on his knees, recited the Hail Mary, which much impressed Shun-chih. The conversation continued. Suddenly the emperor broke in: 'But, *Ma-fa,* I have been here many hours and you have offered me nothing to eat or drink.' Schall excused himself by asking what he could place before him that would be worthy of the emperor. 'Give me a little wine,' said Shun-chih. Schall at once presented him with a glass of the red wine of Shensi which came in this instance from the vines of the Fathers there; and also with wine bought from Dutch merchants. The emperor would have none of either; instead he savoured with pleasure that which Schall himself had made from grapes of the vine which overhung the window of his room. While sipping the product of its fruits, Shun-chih looked through the window at the vine with its newly swelling grapes. 'In a few months,' said he, 'when they are ripe, I will come and taste them.' In such a way did Shun-chih rest and refresh himself with his friend, after all the troubles of ruling an empire. In the midst of his birthday celebrations on March 15, 1657, he announced to the gathered dignitaries that he wished to keep the day at Schall's residence. Schall was of the company and he had to make all haste home in order to furnish a suitable welcome.

Shun-chih witnessed his respect and affection by impulsive gestures and striking favours. When he sat on the raised imperial throne he did not allow Adam Schall to remain sitting on the floor along with other notables; he had to come up a step, an honour reserved for the nearest relatives in the imperial family. He often presented Schall with a bowl of Manchu tea (which, unlike Chinese tea, has milk added to it) from which he himself had first drunk. It especially pleased him to do this in front of officials and great men of higher rank than that of Schall to show plainly where his preference lay. He was skilful in the chase. Once, having shot his quarry at full gallop, he presented the hare to Schall with the words: 'This will be an excellent jugged hare as a treat for my *Ma-fa.*' Another time he gave him two fans (a great feature, of course, of Chinese

life) painted with his own hands, while a very high official murmured in Schall's ear that he would have given two thousand
gold pieces for such a present. A cold day found the emperor
and Schall together; in the middle of the conversation Shun-
chih took off his fur cloak clasped with gold and with a gesture
of familiar affection placed it round the shoulders of his friend.

There were also public honours. As Director of the Institute
of Astronomy Schall received a salary two thirds greater than
that of a minister of state; the emperor wanted to raise this still
further but was dissuaded at Schall's earnest request. The fifth
class of officials to which Schall belonged was thought to be
insufficiently exalted. During the regency, in 1646, he had been
given the title of vice-president of the Institute of Imperial
Sacrifices which raised him to the fourth rank. On September
15, 1651, three honours were conferred on him at once, one
of them giving him the right to rank as a mandarin of the highest
division of the third class. On April 2, 1653, an official document, probably dictated by the emperor himself, conferred on
him the title of Master Who Searches Out Celestial Secrets;
and this was inscribed also on the column erected outside the
church Schall had built. Finally, after still more honours, Adam
Schall became on February 2, 1658, Grand Officer of the Imperial Banquets, or the Imperial Chamberlain we might say.
This automatically raised him to the rank of mandarin of the
highest division of the first class, equal to the emperor's chief
councillors and the greatest princes of the imperial family. He
wore from now on the insignia of this rank: the button made
from a red gem on his hat and the crane with spread wings
embroidered in gold on the breast of his gown. Not content with
this the emperor, following Chinese custom, conferred honours
on Adam Schall's parents and grandparents (in 1651), and
later as far back as the third generation.

Father Schall accepted these honours. In the first place, he
was able in his privileged position to gain the interest of the

emperor, delighted to do something for his *Ma-fa*, for the benefit of others.

Schall's first care was for those working under him. Thanks to him, the astronomical institute itself was made more comfortable, while the wages of its employees were raised and in 1655 sixteen new observers were added to the four who were finding the work a good deal too much for them. The cold could become intense, and Schall obtained wool coats for all those working for him and saw to it that they had a larger supply of coal. His concern extended to the individual. For the son of one of the poorer workmen who died in 1658 he obtained an imperial grant to enable him to give his father the fitting (and elaborate) funeral so dear to the Chinese soul. It is clear from the many and various petitions and requests he made to the emperor that Father Schall, the Director of the Institute of Astronomy, was indeed a father in his care, physical and spiritual, for those for whom he was responsible.

His work for the poor was not neglected, above all in times of famine or other distress. There was an epidemic of smallpox in Peking, made worse by the hunger which sapped people's resistance. Typically, Father Schall saw a sign of divine disfavour in this: the emperor had been flirting with the lamas, Buddhist priests or monks of Tibet. Equally typically, the 'reparation' was as practical a one as could be devised, bearing in mind that no real cure was known for the disease itself—the really large sum of 400,000 *taels* was distributed to the poor of the city. The following year, unusually heavy rains brought flooding to Peking and its neighbourhood. Once again Schall intervened with the authorities, and the government granted 800,000 *taels* to the miserable victims in Peking and 240,000 to those in the surrounding countryside.

As in the large and complex states of the modern West, unemployment was a conspicuous problem. In this, too, Adam

Schall took an interest, pressing for the rebuilding of Peking, ravaged by the fires of the revolution, the rebuilding of the palace also and the improvement of the city walls. This proposal was quickly put into operation. At the same time, Schall was concerning himself with the fortunes of prisoners and those in the hands of the authorities. Some Peking merchants had been sentenced to death and their fortunes confiscated. But this wealth, instead of going to the treasury, had found its way into the pockets of certain officials. Encouraged by such success, they had other merchants imprisoned who were innocent of any crime. On learning of this Schall at once informed the emperor and the unfortunate men were freed on the same day. During one period of widespread unrest and distress, Schall asked for and obtained a general amnesty.

The emperor himself provoked another unhappy situation in which Father Schall intervened to everyone's benefit. Shun-chih had conceived one of those fantastic notions which came to him from time to time. There was to be a great hunting expedition organized north of Peking along the Great Wall; the nobles were to provide the horses and retinues of the poor would be needed for the service of both men and beasts. There was general murmuring at the project as the peasants foresaw their only too probably wretched existence, possibly even death, in the harsh border country. Father Schall took himself to the emperor to remonstrate. 'What?' said Shun-chih, 'Do you know I have been discussing this expedition with my nobles and governors for months? And they all approve of it.' 'Naturally,' Schall replied. 'Would they dare gainsay the emperor? But among the poor people, who do not possess warm clothes or arms or horses, there is not one who does not disapprove. Look, sire, at the hovels on the outskirts of the city, without fire or food and exposed to all the winds that blow. If the misery of these people is great now, what will it be out in the wilds? . . . I beg you on my knees to change your wishes for all our sakes.

Before compelling the people into needless excursions let them have what they stand in need of at home; then you, the emperor, will be well watched over.' Shun-chih allowed Schall to go home without a reply to this. But in the evening the horses were returned to their owners; the expedition was given up.

In 1653, Adam Schall was able to save from death no fewer than two hundred Manchu noblemen. It was the custom that when a prince of the imperial house died on the battlefield all his chief officers must die too, unless they could prove that they had been absent from the battle on the express orders of the prince. Such an occasion arose. A prince was killed in the south, victim in fact of his own rashness, and although the victory was afterwards gained, two hundred officers and four governors were sentenced to death. Schall was the only person who dared raise his voice to ask for mercy. He was to some extent involved already, as he had advised the emperor against choosing that particular prince as a general of his army. The emperor's response to his plea was immediate: 'Once again it is only you who understand my inmost wishes. I myself want to extend mercy to these men; but I am still but a young man and I was afraid of impairing military discipline. I remember your previous advice. If heaven's wishes are thus and thus, why should we lay the blame on human beings?' The officers and officials were set at liberty, receiving, to fulfil the demands of punishment, a degradation in rank.

Schall gives us many more instances of the emperor's truly filial behaviour towards himself; and he tells us also of the change in the attitude of Shun-chih's mother until she appeared almost as attached to him as was her son. At the very first this was by no means so. She was a great patron of the lamas and highly suspicious of Schall, all contact with whom she avoided. Her attitude changed suddenly, and as early as 1651. The emperor was away hunting with most of the young nobility, leaving the palace to his mother and the palace

officials. Schall was greatly surprised when three ladies sent
from the emperor's mother appeared at his residence. Her
'daughter' had been gravely sick for some days, they said, and
she had no confidence in any doctor except the European priest;
nothing was hidden from him, she was sure, and what was his
counsel? Schall of course knew nothing of the nature of the
disease, and he took one of his straightforward steps which
so often look like naivety to a sophisticated mind. He prayed,
then gave the ladies some *Agnus Dei* asking that they should be
placed on the sick girl. He said, daringly again it might seem,
'The sickness will be cured in four days.' And so it was. Within
that time the 'daughter', who in fact was the emperor's be-
trothed, recovered her health. The grateful mother showered
gifts on Father Schall and maintained that from now on he must
consider her as his 'child'. While thanking her with gentle
courtesy for such kindnesses, Schall took the opportunity to
suggest that she should no longer extend such marked favour to
the Buddhist priests which, he said, 'was leading the people
astray'. She agreed to withdraw her patronage from them
gradually.

It was now her aim to render Adam Schall any service, great
or small. When, for example, she learned by chance that he
was wishing for an ox for his farm she at once sent him two
magnificent beasts. Schall could not give her greater pleasure
than by turning to her with some request.

In return for such benevolence, Father Schall's one desire
was to give the emperor and his mother the supreme gift of
Christianity. But his hopeful spirit did not blind him to the
fact that this could be done neither easily nor quickly. He saw
clearly that the young emperor must first learn to take the inter-
mediate steps. Before Shun-chih could become a Christian he
must learn to be a man; before anything of the character, the
'law', of the spiritual life could be set before him, he must be

taught and must accept the fullness of natural law, concerning the nature of man as man. In Schall's view, and it is of some importance, this is the only road of approach to a genuine conversion. 'A true conversion,' he remarks, 'does not just affect outward actions, the exterior; it essentially involves thoughts and emotions. Philip did not ask the eunuch of Queen Candace whether he believed, but whether he believed "with all his heart" [Acts 8 : 37]. Many people,' Schall goes on, 'keep some attachment hidden away in a corner of their hearts of a kind which a genuine faith must condemn. They believe in God's word, accept his commandments. But, through some spiritual habit, long indulged passion or subtle indifference, they refuse to give over their whole heart to God. This is even more true with people of the East. Their conversion is not really genuine unless God's grace in them is almost superabounding, the Father drawing them in spite of themselves. While the neophyte regards even God's Commandments of the Old Law with displeasure and while he has still no real wish to relinquish those things which are standing in the way, then there is no point in trying to proceed further. The first object in the work of winning men to Christianity must be the removal of these obstacles.'

In accordance with these clear and valuable principles, Schall's first efforts were to encourage the young emperor to be a 'man of reason', a rational being, before any idea should necessarily arise that he might become also a man of faith. Schall's task was to teach him to conquer his caprices, his lusts and superstitions: to comport himself, that is, like a true king, with his first concern the happiness and prosperity of his country.[1]

---

[1] Ideas in our own time are not always clear about this distinction between what may be demanded of man by nature and reason and what by faith. Their correspondence to reality is reflected in the fact that what Adam Schall is asking of the emperor here were largely commonplaces in the higher moral and philosophical teachings of pagan Greece and Rome and, indeed, in pure Confucianism.

Adam Schall knew Shun-chih; it was to him that the young
man most freely revealed his moods of thoughtlessness and
stubbornness, and general instability. His method was to instruct the emperor, as a teacher would a young child, by simple
details and examples: 'Don't gallop headlong after your game
like a young barbarian; don't wander in lonely and perhaps
dangerous places; don't play about with the fire-arms which the
Dutch have imported into China, one careless slip and there
could be a fatal accident.'

On one occasion in particular he was able to deal with an
instance of the emperor's lack of self control which might well
have proved disastrous. A powerful pirate called Ch'eng-kung,
long an enemy of the Manchus, had seized some islands in the
mouth of the Yangtze-kiang. In 1659 he sailed up river with
a sizeable fleet and laid siege to Nanking, the southern capital,
which was defended by five thousand soldiers of whom the only
dependable troops were five hundred Manchus. Forces were
sent to raise the siege, but these were destroyed by Ch'eng-
kung's savage band, and it seemed certain that Nanking would
fall. When he heard the news the emperor lost his head and,
panic-stricken, wanted to take refuge in Manchuria. His mother
reasoned with him, pointing out the shame and cowardice of
abandoning so feebly the country valiantly won by his people.
He thereupon made one of his about turns and drawing a sword
he declared: 'I will go myself to the battlefield and either conquer or die!' Then he proceeded to hack the imperial throne to
pieces, crying: 'This will be the fate of those who dare oppose
my purpose!' His mother failed to calm him. Another lady,
once his nurse, who had retained great influence over the young
man, was no more successful; indeed she fled before his flashing
blade. Consternation reigned; if the emperor should flee or
should be killed by the enemies of the state it would in all prob-
ability mean the fall of Manchu power. With one accord,
princes, nobles, court officials turned to Father Schall, begging

him, one after the other, to intervene. This was a question of
direct interference in the political affairs of the country and
Schall did not at once consent. However, he finally discussed it
with two other Fathers, drew up his formal petition, said Mass
with especial fervour for God's blessing on his undertaking and
set out for the palace. His fellows in the Jesuit residence were
moved even to tears, for they all knew that, in spite of Schall's
relationship with Shun-chih, to come between the emperor and
his passions on this matter could cost Schall his life.

Schall was told when he arrived that the emperor seemed a
little calmer. He was introduced into his presence and, kneeling,
he presented the petition, entreating Shun-chih not to bring his
empire to its downfall. 'I would rather be cut in pieces than fail
in this, my duty,' he said. The young man's face changed as
Schall's steadfastness and courage struck him. He courteously
raised him, saying: 'I know that my *Ma-fa* cares only for my
good.' The news spread abroad and was received like that of a
victory: 'The emperor is not going.' On Schall's advice a
fresh force was dispatched, which drove the pirates and their
leader back to their island stronghold. Adam Schall was hailed
as 'saviour of the Empire'. Many distinguished men came to the
residence to thank him, honouring him and his companions with
the deeply respectful greeting of the *k'ou t'ou*.

The emperor's often ungovernable nature led him into all the
wildness of almost brutish lusts. Here Schall did not hesitate
to make his voice heard. Before the emperor's marriage, some
particularly distressing reports reached Schall and he at once
presented himself at the palace and remonstrated with Shun-
chih. The young man was trembling with a mixture of rage and
shame, and he refused to listen. As if giving him up in despair,
Schall made to retire from the emperor's presence, but he was
called back. Abashed and confused, the emperor asked him always to bring him back to a right path: 'I *will* listen to you;
and I promise to amend my ways if I have really done wrong.'

To emphasize this 'reconciliation' he invited Schall to eat with him, showing him anew many signs of favour.

Once again, some time after the royal marriage, Father Schall considered it necessary to visit the young emperor and this time to admonish him severely, recalling his former counsels and not desisting until he succeeded in making the young man red with shame. The emperor had certainly been thinking over Schall's lessons, for he then ventured on a query.

'Tell me, *Ma-fa*, which is the greater sin, lust or avarice?' Schall had had occasion to rebuke him for this other of the 'deadly sins', and he replied, 'Avarice embitters men, and makes them each other's enemies, above all when it leads to fraud and cruelty. But this sin is more directly an insult to God than a crime against men. Lust, on the contrary, especially when its example is given by the great, is highly infectious and is therefore the more dangerous. But they are both mortal sins, and lead to eternal death.'

The emperor nodded his head in approval of this little excerpt from Catholic moral theology; he asked Schall to come and talk with him often and again entertained him at the imperial table before his departure.

The Tartars were if anything more under the sway of superstitious customs than the Chinese, and here Shun-chih certainly showed himself one of his race. Evil spirits, bad omens, the shades of their ancestors, all these could strike terror into their lives and impel them into this or that rite or observance. These fears subjected them to the influence of the lamas, who thus wielded real power.

Lamaism—of Tibet, Mongolia and northern China—often appears to us in innocent and even touching guise; but it is in fact an impure form of Buddhism, one which has been distorted by a highly developed demonology derived from Tibetan popular beliefs. The mass of rites and sacrifices practised by the lamas are intended to appease or win the favour of the in-

numerable spirits which are imagined to inhabit the gloomy
and threatening mountain ranges. Lamas may have something
of both the magician and the prophet in them while the ancestor worship, which plays an essential part, is not to be confused with the really respectable customs of Chinese Confucianism. There is an elaborate priestly hierarchy, with the
Grand Lama (no doubt the representative of Lamaism best
known in the West) at its head. He lives, or should live[1], in the
famous Tibetan monastery at Lhasa and is both religious and
civil head of the country. His prestige is immense. All is holy
about him, for it is in him that Buddha has chosen to be re-
incarnated. In fact, since the time of Tsongkapa in the fifteenth
century there have been two chief lamas, two reincarnations of
aspects of the Buddha: the Dalai Lama at Lhasa ('the powerful: he who resembles the ocean') and a second, lesser in fame
and influence, who lives in the monastery at Tashi Lumpo. It
was with the first of these that Schall came in contact.

When the Tartars became masters of China the influence of
the Dalai Lama spread with them. Indeed, his wish was for the
emperor to declare himself his disciple publicly and officially.
Lamas resided in Peking, their head claimed a kingly title
and was borne in royal fashion on the shoulders of his disciples.
As we have seen, the emperor's mother had favoured them;
while an uncle and a half-brother of Shun-chih remained their
devoted supporters. Their hope was wholly to gain over the
young emperor who had already made them a grant of a million
pieces of gold to enable them to erect temples and other buildings. Adam Schall was well aware of the situation, and he decided to wage war on their influence.

His petitions and counsel were aimed at showing the em-

[1] The present Dalai Lama, of course, fled to India in 1959 when Chinese
forces occupied Tibet. Reports tell us of attempts to destroy Tibetan religion;
but, as in China itself, it seems highly improbable that, at least as yet, this
has had any profound impact on the age-old customs of a widely scattered
peasantry inured to hardships of all kinds.

peror the worthlessness of their pretensions: 'It is their boast
that they drive out demons, bring health, cure the sick by
charms. This is all a delusion. It is the practice of virtue which
brings victory over evil spirits; through the power of Almighty
God they are rendered harmless.' Their threats are as vain as
their promises: 'They say that if the emperor does not declare
himself their disciple he will die within the year, during the
eighth month. These false prophets are deceiving you. God
alone knows the future. Are we to suppose that these ignorant
and boorish men have somehow managed to gain admittance
to the councils of the Most High? For my part I very much hope
that, with God's blessing, you will reign for many years yet.'[1]

The lamas tried also to scare the emperor through ancestor
worship. 'If the emperor does not want to displease the shades
of his ancestors,' they said, 'he must make a pilgrimage into the
province of Liaotung [in Manchuria] where his father and
grandfather are buried, to thank them for the great extension
of his kingdom.' Respectful of the lamas, and fearing to fail in
his duty, Shun-chih prepared to obey. The day on which he
was to set out was already decided when Schall remonstrated
that this journey was being regarded by the people as a kind
of flight: 'The news is going round that the emperor is giving
up the rule of his great empire in favour of taking his ease in a
few outlying provinces. The lamas know this. Those who are
recommending this journey are nearly all from the province of
Shensi which is always in a state of unrest; they want to see the
emperor as far away as possible so that they can the better
organize opposition to him. Send representatives to offer sacrifice at the tombs of your ancestors; but do yourself remain at
Peking to govern the empire.' This time Schall had to return
to the charge twice before the emperor came round to his view.

[1] We may note, especially in relation to evil spirits, Schall's precise orthodoxy
here. Evil spirits exist (though perhaps not in the exact form of popular
belief); God has power over them; but man is required to play his part by
'faith and good works'.

The Dalai Lama now came to the conclusion that the only thing to do was to make a personal appearance in Peking. He reinforced the influence which might be supposed to flow from his presence by arranging an escort of three thousand lamas and thirty thousand Mongolian supporters. Urged on no doubt by the local lamas, Shun-chih proposed to go to the frontier to meet him. Thereupon Father Schall obtained an audience and managed to persuade the emperor not to take this step: 'It is not fitting that so great a monarch should pay such honour to a lama from outside his kingdom; it would be a lasting disgrace for himself and a lamentable example for his descendants.' After this, the emperor's uncle and half-brother tried in vain to move him, and it was finally arranged that the uncle should receive the distinguished guest at the city gates. In the meantime the emperor would be hunting in a wood near by and would then greet him as it were casually; this obviated the awkward situation of the emperor himself introducing a foreigner into his own palace. In due time the Grand Lama was formally received, Shun-chih sitting on a raised throne surrounded by nobles and representatives of other countries. He politely rose, gave his guest his hand and offered him a place among the high officials. But he refused to declare himself his disciple or accede to other of his wishes. After some days, the Grand Lama was bidden a polite farewell, rewarded handsomely with money and other presents, and he went home to his own country.

As if encouraged by his own steady and statesmanlike behaviour, the emperor now exiled to the same province of Liaotung to which the lamas had tried to inveigle him the chief lama in Peking, he who had had the audacity to use a royal title just outside the emperor's own palace. The lamas of course knew that it was Schall who so constantly stood in their path; he was execrated as a particularly hostile sorcerer.

It gave Adam Schall great satisfaction to see the success, if only partial, of his endeavours to free the young emperor from the irrational fears which beset him. The results of his work were apparent on one very difficult occasion in 1657. It was the eve of the emperor's birthday, and he had gone to the Jesuit residence to have one of his long talks with his *Ma-fa*. In the compound some blacksmiths were employed, and after a time Shun-chih, who had been half listening to the rhythm of their hammer blows, desired to go out and see them at work. On his appearance the workmen, astonished and even alarmed, stopped dead. When told to continue their work, one of them placed a piece of white hot iron on the anvil and struck it with such enthusiasm that a shower of sparks flew out over the emperor. In trying to avoid them he leapt to one side and stumbled over a ten foot deep drain which had been hidden by a pile of rushes; very fortunately he managed not to fall in. The men were thunderstruck and terrified; quite apart from prospects of immediate punishment such an accident was taken as an omen of calamity. Schall himself fell on his knees asking his guest's pardon for the incivility and his carelessness; but at the same time he begged the emperor not to regard the accident as a sign of evil to come, even though it was on the eve of his birthday. Shun-chih was quite calm; he simply remarked that everyone's foot slipped at one time or another: 'It is of no importance, *Ma-fa*. Do not distress yourself over so little.'

In his efforts to form young Shun-chih into a man, master of himself, and thus a good ruler, Schall laid great emphasis on a monarch's duty to give a good example. One day the emperor asked why most of the governors and officials were so negligent of affairs of state, especially when they were so indulgently treated. Schall's reply struck home: 'It is my belief that it is because they all imitate your example, Sire. They observe that you yourself deal with such things lightly, as if you did not have the well-being of the state really at heart.' More than once Schall had advised Shun-chih not to leave the concerns of the empire solely to the governing officials. To the example given by his own hard work, the emperor should join real prudence, above all when it is a question of choosing those who help him in his task of governing. He should test and know thoroughly those whom he wished to employ, so as to be able to set aside the doubtful characters, the unreliable and the lazy, and also those officials who are too proud or too old—impatient of counsel or unable to adapt themselves. A monarch worthy of the name should love his people, be easily approachable and do good with pleasure. While prudent, he should be also magnanimous. Over the question of the two hundred Manchu officers, Schall observed to the emperor: 'Let us admit that they may not be exempt from all fault; would it not still be better for them and of more use to the State to give them an opportunity to make amends for their negligence?' On one occasion when Schall was speaking of these things the emperor declared that he felt like a man woken from sleep, and he promised henceforward to take affairs of state much more seriously.

We find these admonitions of Schall's making their mark on the little homilies which Shun-chih addressed to his various officials. It became a custom of the Manchu emperors to encourage and instruct their subordinates in this way, and more than two hundred small volumes of these exhortations have come down to us, six being those of Shun-chih. In many of them we can plainly see the expression of Schall's teachings. We may echo the words written about Father Schall as long ago as 1847: 'During the whole reign of Shun-chih Schall was, without the title thereof, one of the most powerful ministers of state in China.'

Adam Schall tells us of how, when the opportunity offered, he gradually moved on from this fundamental building up of the young ruler's character to the consideration of the 'mysteries' of Christ and the supernatural virtues demanded by the Gospel. One of their most interesting conversations took place in 1656. It was nightfall. The emperor had returned from hunting and was surrounded by his nobles and eunuchs, while through the palace windows the shining stars could be seen. Father Schall arrived to present a report to the emperor who glanced over it and then looked up.

'Tell me,' he said. 'If the courses of the stars are predetermined, if they are inevitable, then aren't the misfortunes which they presage inevitable and inescapable too?'

'The movements of the stars are indeed fixed from our viewpoint,' replied Schall. 'But God who has determined them is free; and he has done so in such a manner as to give men and especially rulers due warning of their duties and responsibilities.'

'Who is God, who has done all this?'

'He can not be seen, but he is almighty and has created all things, visible and invisible. He is not an idol made with hands, nor indeed is he those heavens which we can see, but the infinite Lord. Everywhere he is present and he knows all things; Christians call him after the most noble of his creations: *T'ien-chu*—Lord of the Heavens, or, better still, the Creator.'

The emperor was still mulling over the weight of Chinese astrological tradition, without perhaps quite realizing what was disturbing him. Schall, following his constant policy, tried to build up on this, not to destroy it by a frontal attack. Shunchih's next question, then, was: 'But why do I have to be more concerned about the evils which may threaten than are other monarchs?'

To which the reply ran: 'Because you are the first of sovereigns in the world.' This was of course the normal Chinese view, and indeed in most ways was true enough. 'Do you not call yourself the Son of Heaven? Are there not more people under your rule than under that of any other monarch? This is why God grants you this especial care, though of course he does not neglect other kings.'

'And if I banish my faults will that mean that the evils threatening me will be removed?'

'The movements and position of the stars will be unchanged; but you yourself will have nothing to fear.'

It is probable that the emperor took this much more simply than Schall's measured answer might imply. Certainly, his response was immediate.

'Very well, then. *Ma-fa*, teach me how to free myself from my sins!'

'You must begin by modifying the rigour of your law sometimes; watch over your people like a father; encourage, commend and generally treat better those who help you to govern. In other words, follow the rule of doing to others as you would wish them to do to yourself. Then all will go well.'

Schall went on to set forth the Ten Commandments to the young man, laying especial emphasis on their relation to the duties of the sovereign. When he had listened with great attention, Shun-chih asked: 'Are they many in China who observe this doctrine?'

'No, not very many. But of those who do the great majority keep the law of God with all their hearts. If a number do commit serious faults, it is often because the authorities in China do not restrain evil-doers to the extent that is customary in Europe.'

A little later, the young emperor came back to the question which was clearly much on his mind.

'Are sovereigns expected to observe these commandments, like everyone else?'

'Even more; for it is they who have to give an example to their subjects.'

'Even I, who am not a Christian?'

It must be remembered that the subject under discussion here was the Commandments of the Old Law, the law of 'natural man', to which the Christian revelation was both additional and a fulfilment. Schall's orthodox reply therefore was: 'These commandments are binding on all men. A man who follows such a rule of life earns eternal life; he who purposely violates them merits eternal punishment.'

'But what fortitude is required to make such enormous efforts.'

'Nothing is hard for the person who really tries, with God's help.'

'Then I will try to live in this way,' was the emperor's conclusion; 'for I think what you say is true, and I believe I can accomplish what is necessary.'

Sometimes in conversations of this kind, the emperor asked for further enlightenment on the name and nature of God; or he would inquire about the work of Christian apostleship among his people; or again he asked for an explanation of the Apostle's Creed which he commanded to be written down. He sat up till dawn reading expositions of Christian doctrine written in Chinese by the Jesuit Fathers. He also came across the fine manuscript which Schall had presented to Ch'ung-chên, looked through it and asked Schall to tell him about its contents. Schall gave him an account of the life of Christ, but when he approached the story of the Passion the emperor rose from his seat and knelt down, and thus he remained until all was told. Schall comments on this: 'I have often given a similar account to the highly educated or the scholars; and their pride saw it as an act of folly that any one should suffer in this way for us. They listened inattentively or laughed. But this great sovereign fell to his knees with such humility and listened with such feeling that I could scarcely restrain my tears.'

Shun-chih showed the same kind of interest when he visited the Jesuit residence. He would go into the chapel, carefully read the tablets on the walls and ask about the lives of the saints whose statues were there. On one occasion he stopped before the tabernacle, bowed his head and struck his breast. But in spite of all these striking signs of good will, Adam Schall did not expect an immediate conversion. The flowering of faith required

more time and deeper thought. The emperor himself sent back
to Schall a picture of the image of the Holy Face on the veil
of Veronica, with the message that he was not yet of a right
disposition fittingly to honour this sorrowful image of the
Saviour. Yet, if time, thought and prayer were still required,
it seemed that the end was certain. In fact, Father Schall was
to be left with the consolation that he had done all that could
have been done. The time was to come when some would re-
proach him with having essentially played only a walking-on part
in the drama of life at court. He replied without false humility:
'I have never been ashamed of the Gospel, before the emperor
or anyone else. I used every opportunity to make it known.'

In a letter early in the year 1661, Father Verbiest declared:
'Father Schall exercises an influence with the emperor possessed
by neither viceroy nor prince.' The advantages of this for the
mission in China may be imagined.

One of Schall's services was to help to ensure that the Calvinist Dutch did not effectively enter the empire. They had
taken their check at Macao in their stride, and continued to
work for power in the East. In occupation of the key position
of Malacca (once Portuguese), they now held virtually the
monopoly of trade with Japan and hoped to gain the same
privileges in China; two references to Dutch merchandise have
already suggested their activities. The governor of Batavia,
John Maatzuiker, undertook the negotiation of a trade agreement with the emperor in the years 1653-54, but this came to
nothing. Two years later, another mission was organized, led by
Peter van Goyer and James de Keyser. This one seemed to
possess all the elements of success: exterior pomp, valuable
gifts and plenty of money. They certainly worked wonders at
Canton; the two governors were quite won over and they gave
the mission official permission to proceed to Peking, at the same
time condescending to re-cast in the proper Chinese form the
letter being carried from the Dutch governor to the emperor.

First contacts with ministers at Peking were also highly promising; here again relations were facilitated by handsome presents.

Some months previously, on February 13, Adam Schall had warned the emperor against such visitors. 'The Dutch,' he explained, 'are rebels who have rejected the authority of their legitimate king and since then they have been infesting the high seas. Wherever they settle they put up fortifications, and from these extend their power and trouble their neighbours. It would not be good to conclude a trading treaty with them.'[1] Schall was informed on July 30 when the mission arrived. His first observation was that most of the gifts were not Dutch at all, but the produce of other countries; and he remarked that the visitors gave the impression of treating the emperor like the head of a business firm.

'All the same,' broke in Shun-chih, raising a question which has haunted Christian missionary endeavours ever since those times, 'the Dutch are Christians.'

Schall replied with the directness of his personality and of his period.

'Yes. But in name only. They have rebelled against God and against their king. The authorities there will confirm that in the second year of the reign of the emperor T'ien-ch'i the Dutch attempted to take Macao, which pays you tribute. I was there, and played a part in repulsing them. Two years ago they wished to present themselves before you to offer tribute in the name of their own ruler. They were not admitted because they did not have credentials. Now they claim to have them. This can't be so: the voyage to Holland and back would take thirty-two months, as well as the eight months for the return journey from

---

[1] Adam Schall had not been brought up on English history books! For the sake of the more comprehensive view it should not perhaps be forgotten that while there was support for the revolt of the Spanish Netherlands in England (as on the Continent, where Spain was not especially popular), Elizabeth I herself, sensitive about rebellion against sovereign rulers, did not look on it with a markedly favourable eye.

Peking to Canton. This disingenuousness alone should put you on your guard; but it also reveals the intentions of the Dutch. They are less interested in arranging a trade agreement than in gaining a foothold in China.'

Negotiations continued for some time without the Dutch gaining any particular benefit. Finally, on October 14, the imperial decision was communicated to them: every eight years they would be permitted to send a mission to Peking to pay tribute to the emperor, and on that occasion goods might be bought and sold. Two hours later they set out on their homeward journey. They attributed their failure to gain anything more substantial to the Jesuits, and Schall had certainly intervened; but it seems unlikely that the emperor would ever have given them the same privileges as the Portuguese at Macao. Holland was already too powerful in the East; her capture of Formosa from Portugal had brought her sufficiently close to China without encouraging further pretensions. Indeed the Portuguese themselves were in danger of being turned out and losing their trading rights. It was Schall who pacified Shun-chih and obtained an imperial decree confirming the Portuguese in Macao.

'We all preach the Gospel in the beneficent shadow of Schall's reputation,' wrote the Polish Father Smogulechi in 1652, and this was true no less of the Dominicans and Franciscans who had entered China in the Jesuits' footsteps. One of Schall's services was precisely to facilitate the entry of missionaries into the empire; in July 1658, for instance, fourteen Jesuit Fathers arrived together. Two who were mathematicians had the expenses of their journey paid for them and were officially escorted to Peking. Nine Dominicans were likewise given entry. The emperor would have liked to see twenty Jesuit Fathers in Peking itself, but failing that he was most generous to those who were there. He gave them a larger residence, with better grounds and more flourishing gardens; and also made them a formal gift of the place where Matthew Ricci was buried. Adam Schall obtained a piece of ground adjoining for his own burial place. The Jesuits in Peking were able to support four more missionaries, thanks to benefactions from the emperor.

Great freedom was granted for the preaching of the Gospel throughout the empire. These privileges could be a kind of restriction; when another Polish Father wished to journey north into the lands of the Tartars the emperor did not approve: 'You have all my empire before you; travel in it where you wish, preaching the doctrine of heaven in the way that seems best to you.' Governors and other officials were pleased to do a service for Father Schall's colleagues. In his account of these times, published in Vienna in 1673, Father John Gabiani says: 'To enter the country freely, to be esteemed by mandarins, officials and the populace, to enjoy the freedom to preach as of a right, the missionary of whatever Order need only to present himself as a companion or connection of Father Schall.' His name more than once saved his brethren from trouble and worse. A certain Father de Ferrariis was condemned to ten strokes of the bastinado and then to be exiled; why, we do not now know. But an onlooker spoke up and bore witness that the prisoner was one of the companions of T'ang Jo-wang. The Jesuit was at once set free with apologies.

More curious was the affair of Father Ludovic Buglio and Father Gabriel de Magalhães. For this we must go back to the revolt of Chang Hsien-chung against the new imperial dynasty, mentioned in the previous chapter. This adventurer seized the province of Szechwan in whose capital, Chengtu, the two Jesuits were working. They fled, but were brought back and compelled to serve their new master. Chang had his generous impulses and was not a stranger to arts and education; but his instincts were barbarous and bloodthirsty. He terrorized the two men; sometimes treating them with fulsome respect, promising to build numbers of Christian churches when he ruled the empire, at others abusing them as foreigners and threatening to send them and all the missionaries back to Europe.

Chang declared himself king and emperor and marched to subdue the province of Shensi. His method of ensuring that there should be no uprising behind his back in Szechwan was to carry out an appalling massacre, 40,000 victims in Chengtu alone. The two Jesuit Fathers were made his companions, and had to stand by and watch his savageries. They repeatedly asked to be released; and they firmly refused to accede to his demand to worship as he did. Father de Magalhães most courageously met his threats with: 'We are members of a religious order, and worship the one God. Though we are innocent, you speak of putting us to death; but be sure, within a few days the God you deny would punish you to the full.' This impressed Chang for the moment, but a few days later they were condemned to die. At almost the last moment however, on January 3, 1647, news came that the first soldiers of a Manchu army sent out to crush the rebels were in sight. Chang Hsien-chung was no general; he mounted his horse and rode madly towards the enemy troops, apparently to get a closer look at them. He fell, with a Tartar arrow through his heart. His leaderless army scattered in disorder; the two Jesuit Fathers tried to escape, but were wounded by the conquerers' arrows and captured.

They were regarded as enemy prisoners. Death by beheading seemed still in store for them. However, when they were brought before the Manchu general in the evening he was struck by their beards, unlike the Chinese fashion yet reminiscent of someone. He asked whether they knew anything of T'ang Jo-wang. 'He is our "brother"!' exclaimed de Magalhães. Thereupon the prisoners were taken back to their tent and treated with much respect. Father Magalhães wrote later to Schall: 'Our blessings on the Calendar! It has saved our lives.' Unfortunately this gratitude was not to survive further and unforeseen trials.

This story will find its completion when we come to consider the character of Father Schall and other people's reactions to it, especially those with whom he worked as a missionary.

One other brief mention may be made of a similar service. A Father Antony, a Franciscan, had been accused of espionage, Schall was able to save him too; and the Franciscan wrote to his provincial in the Philippines full of praise and recognition of Schall's services in China, and asking that his benefactor might be sent some finest linen albs for Mass on great feasts.

As might be expected, the numbers converted to Christianity were exceptionally high during these times. Father Verbiest speaks of ten thousand a year. According to Father Gabiani the number of baptisms (children of Christian parents and new converts) in the years 1651 to 1664 was 104,940; while in 1663 the visitor apostolic gives the number of Christians in China as 140,000. It is interesting also to note the fame of Father Schall's rather unusual relations with the Son of Heaven outside the Chinese empire. Father Alexander de Rhodes, who had been a novice with Schall and remained his personal friend and correspondent, writes home to Europe from Indo-China, as do other Jesuits from Macao, describing vividly Schall's success, general popularity and in particular the emperor's extraordinary informality.

We can come no nearer to a triumphant climax. This chapter in Adam Schall's life and in the history of China ends with Shun-chih's death, as historically it should, but not in accordance with Schall's hopes that he should die in the Christian faith. Schall himself had no particular confidence in his own work except in laying the foundations. He had hoped that Father Stephen Le Fèvre would be sent to Peking from the province of Shensi. This Father had a reputation for real holiness; and until recent times at least was still honoured in popular memory in Shensi. But Le Fèvre died in 1657; and from about this time, too, it is noticeable that Schall's influence with the emperor begins to wane. Shun-chih, for all his affection and genuine goodwill, had not the fortitude to break with his own desires, nor with the religious and superstitious powers which surrounded him. He recognized the purity and loftiness of Christianity both by word and deed; but Father Schall might have taken him as an example of the very spiritual condition which he describes so clearly. The stumbling-blocks were too great for the emperor to yield with his whole heart to that grace which spoke to him and drew him. By another common working of spiritual psychology, the young man could not remain where he was. If a person in his situation does not take the final step, then he retreats, gradually or suddenly. Father Schall became aware more or less gradually that his pupil, once affectionate, even loving, was withdrawing his friendship. The breach was widened by a new and dangerous growth in the pernicious influence of the eunuchs who during the regency of the capable Dorgon had been kept well under control.

The emperor had taken to himself the wife of one of the Manchu princes, who had conveniently died or perhaps committed suicide. The young girl became Shun-chih's favourite consort, and when a son was born to her in November, 1657, he was destined for the succession. Three months later the baby died. The position and time of the burial was decided by the stars as was the custom; but the Manchu minister of rites, who was responsible for the ceremonies of the funeral, took it upon himself to change the time in contradiction of the report drawn up by the Institute of Astronomy. The result was that the little prince was buried at an inauspicious hour. This was a disturbance of the order of things, celestial and earthly; and trouble, perhaps disaster, would fall on the imperial family. Two years later the young consort herself died. The minister of rites was

degraded from his position and banished; he nursed his hatred
of Adam Schall for having denounced the false calculations.
There was now no checking the distracted Shun-chih when he
revived a Manchu custom and commanded that thirty ladies
of the late consort's suite should die too, in order that she might
be accompanied in death by a suitable retinue. The whole
empire was to go into mourning; mandarins for a month and
the people for three days. More and more under the influence of
the lamas, Shun-chih thought of becoming a Buddhist monk,
and here Schall was able to aid the emperor's mother in dis-
suading him. But *Ma-fa* was increasingly ignored.

Then Shun-chih fell ill. He was apparently tubercular; but
this was smallpox. Father Schall came to make his last visit to
the emperor, bringing with him a written exhortation on death
and eternal life. The dying man was moved; he felt that T'ang
Jo-wang was indeed his true friend. But, 'he was not worthy to
see God because of his sins'; he still hesitated; when or if he
recovered he would, he said, no doubt accept the doctrine
taught by Schall, but he was too ill at present.

Before he died he called four princes and made a kind of
public confession of his shortcomings. He declared that he had
been neglectful in his government; that often he had not listened
to his mother when she had given him good advice; that he had
not adequately recompensed those who served him, especially
the generals; that he had been financially niggardly towards the
mandarins; that he had not been a father to his people, and that
his grief at the death of his late consort had been uncontrolled
and extravagant. The memory of the many lessons given him
by his *Ma-fa* was still very much alive.

There remained the succession. Shun-chih favoured a cousin;
but his mother and the Manchu princes recommended one of
his sons. For the last time in his life he asked for and listened
to Adam Schall's counsel. He, too, recommended a son, and
the choice was the third of Shun-chih's eight sons, a young

lad of six or seven who was to become K'ang-hsi, one of the greatest of China's emperors, not least in his patronage of Christianity.

Three days later, towards midnight on February 2, 1661, the emperor died. He was not more than twenty-five years old.

The Man and his Work

J ESUITS, Franciscans, Dominicans joined in recognition of
their debt to the Director of the Institute of Astronomy.
But Father Adam Schall by no means escaped criticism. He
possessed indeed the kind of character to which people react
strongly, whether favourably or otherwise; and all through his
life there were those who were provoked into disapproval or
opposition, sometimes violent. There is no need to put this down
at once to obscurantism or unseemly jealousy; rather, we need
to look more closely at Schall himself before coming to any
conclusions.

His vigorous intellect impelled him to take an interest in all
branches of knowledge. Mathematics of course became his
especial concern, but law, biblical studies and history were part
of his ordinary reading. His memory was remarkable; to the
last he could quote from the Classical poets he had read at
school and from an extraordinary variety of other authors. He
had a remarkable gift for languages: he had learned Italian and
Portuguese as well as the usual Greek and Latin; of course, he
spoke Chinese, and he could understand Spanish and Dutch.
His was not the profoundly speculative or philosophic mind,

126

and it was partly natural taste which led him to 'science', in our modern sense of the word. His library, which even before 1651 numbered some three thousand books, would have attracted a priest, or a man of humane learning, but above all a mathematician or astronomer. He was always eager to learn new things (and this was a time of new things in the scientific fields); and yet ready to turn his mind from his distinguished mathematical or astronomical studies to practical works. He cast cannon, constructed scientific apparatus, saw to the building of a church, helped to repair a musical instrument and composed a method by which the novice might learn to play it. In all he did he seemed to be at home, as if that was his particular study or trade in life. Physically, so much work was made possible by his exceptionally robust health which enabled him to do with very little rest and often little sleep. In 1662, when he was seventy, he wrote: 'I suffer from none of the weaknesses of age.'

Schall was not only brilliantly equipped intellectually. We have seen something of his disinterested endeavours and his generosity of temperament; while his loyalty to friends and colleagues withstood some hard blows. His courage was clearly outstanding. At the heart of all this was a religious attitude of the kind which is, sometimes rather confusingly, likened to that of a child; it was childlike, though not childish, in that direct simplicity which is so often found in great men of religion who would be regarded as otherwise learned or even sophisticated. The Director of the Institute of Astronomy was punctilious in saying his daily Mass and never excused himself from any of the Office. The sincere emotionalism of the Rhinelander was seen in his many tears when he preached on the Passion of our Lord or the heroic virtues of the saints. Everywhere and in every incident he saw God's hand, often removing obstacles which stood in the way of his servant's labours or dispersing enemies. With great confidence and often startling results, he made use of the blessed *Agnus Dei*, whether in warding off fire or healing the sick.

The other, and complementary, aspects of these qualities may be seen when his powerful and enthusiastic temperament carried him into quick impulses of pride, trenchant remarks and even dictatorial moments. The conditions of his life, growing old in the relative isolation in which he constantly worked, and often almost entirely on his own responsibility struggling with adversaries in circumstances in which he could not be unaware of his own capabilities, tended to emphasize these traits in his character. Certainly he was not over patient with his superiors (nor does this make him in any way unique!). His language was not guarded. When he exclaimed half-jokingly that after all his only superiors were God and St Ignatius, there were those who were willing to understand this literally—the kind of temperament which can take hard facts in its stride but is disproportionately disturbed by exuberance of speech. More than one of his companions took such sallies amiss. They were shocked, too, at Schall's modifications of the rule of the house for this or that purpose. The step from there to the accusation of being a 'bad religious' is very short in the type of mind which, having embraced 'the rule', proceeds to live by its letter rather than its spirit. What these men murmured to each other became a direct criticism from superiors: 'Father Schall has too many visits and these sometimes at unsuitable times, even at night; he does not pay sufficient attention to the regulation of community life.'

There is no need to feel that Schall is being hardly treated here. While such comments display little appreciation of the work that he was engaged in, it seems highly probable that he to some extent overlooked the needs of the community in the Jesuit residence, even if it was in his character to do so. There is, moreover, no doubt that he was on occasion really imprudent and impatient of remonstrance. Perhaps the most striking example of this is the affair of P'an Chin-hsiao and his young son. P'an was Schall's personal servant, and he had wormed his way into his master's confidence with such success that he was able to repeat round the house various remarks of the kind which Schall should only have made to the most discreet of friends. A certain amount of trouble was caused, and Father Schall was warned about P'an. But by nature careless of idle talk (he was no doubt one of those who say, quite mistakenly, that *words* never hurt anyone), he too hastily put it all down to envious gossip. He went further still. The emperor Shun-chih had been urging his *Ma-fa* to see that his name was perpetuated in future generations, and this could be done by legal adoption which conferred an official's name and title on two or three generations to come. Shun-chih clearly felt deeply about this, and finally Schall agreed. Neither by nature or vocation a respecter of persons, he chose P'an's charming five year old son as his successor according to Chinese law. Schall did in fact take the precaution of choosing the least complete form of adoption; the boy would not inherit fully as by natural right. But he did receive Schall's Chinese 'surname' (spoken first in Chinese) becoming thus T'ang Shih-hung.

The reader may now be awaiting the appearance of the inevitable rumours. As it happens, in Schall's own time his character and way of life were so widely known that neither in his Order nor among the public at large does there seem to have been anything but a common understanding of the facts. This was helped by official recognition of the situation and of the boy himself. In 1661, a decree of the K'ang-hsi, Shun-chih's successor, stated: 'As T'ang Jo-wang has taken a vow of chastity and pledged himself never to marry, and as he must in consequence live sadly like an exile, alone and without support, the emperor [Shun-chih] desired that he should adopt a boy.' The decree then granted to mandarins of high position the privilege of sending a son to the Imperial College which had

9

been established for the education and training of great officials, and it continues: 'T'ang Jo-wang has come from a foreign land and throughout the years has devoted himself to the service of the State. Although he is not married, he is not to be excluded from this privilege; therefore the boy he has adopted is to be admitted to the College. This is a command.' Nevertheless, Schall's action caused misgiving. One result was that it brought him into close contact with P'an Chin-hsiao's extensive family; and his easy-going visits to his home where there were of course many female relatives of all ages, and their return visits to the Jesuit residence, were not in accordance with the sense of propriety of either his colleagues or the stricter Chinese. As for the accusation that the boy was his own son, it came in fact a number of years after Schall's death and played its part in the rather fantastic hostility to the Society of Jesus which was being fomented in Catholic Europe.

Yet Father Schall's patience could be not only exemplary but, in the circumstances, almost extraordinary. We have seen his inch by inch progress at the court of Ch'ung-chên from outside the walls of the imperial palace; the enormous tact and fatherly care in his relationship with Shun-chih. Before going on to complete the history of Father de Magalhães and Father Buglio, which continues to the end of Schall's life and beyond, we may mention a much earlier example.

Among the Franciscans who had been able to take advantage of the Jesuits' breach of the Chinese wall were a certain Father Gaspar Alenda and Father Francis of the Mother of God. They were zealous men with rather more than their share of the Franciscan enthusiasm and simplicity which in the right men and the right circumstances (for instance Father Juniper Serra, the apostle of California) can work such wonders. During the last years of the Ming dynasty, in June 1637, they arrived in Peking and were given hospitality by Father Schall in the Jesuit residence. They were completely ignorant of the world they had

entered, and had made an unfortunate beginning by neglecting
to obtain official permission for the journey at all. Jesuit, and
above all Father Schall's, adaptation to Chinese culture was
for them surrender to idolatry. They wore their Franciscan
habit in public, preached at the most inopportune moments and
exhibited the crucifix whenever they could—the Christian
image which of all others needed gentle and tactful introduction
to the Chinese mentality. Schall tried to explain, to warn them
that they were courting quite unnecessary danger and, with
understanding perhaps of the possibilities of their methods,
suggested that they go to the much less culturally developed
Korea where, moreover, there were as yet no Christians. There
is no record of any impatient word of his, though the harm
they might have done was patent.

Their stay was very short-lived. The authorities, irritated and
doubtless shocked by what was to them a display of barbarian
rudeness, arrested the two men. Having transgressed the law
they might have been severely punished, but through Schall's
skilful intervention they were merely sent back to Fukien
whence they had come. It was not a comfortable or happy
journey, and Father Francis and Father Gaspar long nursed
ill-feeling against the Jesuits who, they were convinced, were at
the back of all their troubles.

Even here, though, it is not without its amusing side to see
that Adam Schall quite unintentionally and indeed innocently
exacerbated the situation. He wrote a highly entertaining personal account of the Franciscans' visit to his friend in Indo-
China, Father de Rhodes. The letter somehow became public
property, and the feeling aroused can be imagined when we read
references to the 'comedy' the worst part of which lay in the
money which had to be found for bribing the Chinese officials;
of the way in which the Jesuit vice-provincial (who had been
in Peking) had dropped these tiresome visitors 'in Schall's lap'
for him to deal with, and how he had been able to be of service

to the Seraphic Father St Francis by saving two of his sons from (quite possible) death.

To return to the unfortunate Father Buglio and Father de Magalhães. After their unwilling involvement with the rebel Chang Hsien-chung and capture by the troops of the new government, their lives, as we have seen, were saved by Adam Schall's name.[1] But they were still prisoners, and were brought to Peking where they were confident of being released. Schall had already considered intervening on their behalf; but his superior Father Furtado, and indeed the captives themselves, had considered that the time was not ripe for this. The position worsened when it became clear that the two Jesuit Fathers were, willy nilly, implicated in the revolt and when the general who had taken them, and who was favourably disposed, fell into disgrace with the regent Dorgon and committed suicide in 1648. At this moment, then, Schall could do nothing for them; and he made matters worse in the eyes of the prisoners by making it clear he thought they had behaved stupidly when in Chang's power and should have refused ever to be seen in his company even if death itself had followed at once. After all, was not Adam Schall himself an official in the service of a Manchu master? This and a good deal more too—the two Fathers, who were now hardly balanced, lent a ready ear to every unfavourable report which came to them, whatever its source—was poured out to whoever would listen to them. That Schall was in fact doing a great deal to ameliorate their captive status, which in time bore very lightly on them so that eventually they were able to exercise their priestly work and even build another Christian church in Peking, meant nothing.

At last their influence had grown so great that three other Jesuit Fathers joined de Magalhães and Buglio in a letter to the vice-provincial, the younger Father Dias, dated May 20, 1649, setting out the reasons why Father Schall should be dismissed

[1] See pp. 120 ff. above.

from the Society of Jesus if he remained recalcitrant. In that case it was suggested that Buglio and de Magalhães should take his place at the Institute of Astronomy. The form of complaint showed a rather simple-minded appreciation of both Schall's temperament and the aims and methods of his work. It was said that he was wanting in obedience and did not observe the poverty of a religious, indeed far from it—he was a mandarin! Schall's informal way of speech, and his equally informal mode of life, also laid him open to unintelligent charges of doubt about his religious orthodoxy and laxity in morals.

All this time Buglio and de Magalhães were in a sense in Father Schall's power. It was his protection which enabled them to be in a position to stir up so much trouble; the difficulty of the circumstances is to be seen in the fact that Father Furtado annoyed the authorities merely by visiting the captives too frequently and was officially ordered out of Peking, an order which, much to Schall's irritation, he did not comply with.

A letter, however, is but a letter. Moreover it reveals something of those who write it. The doubts of Father Dias were confirmed when another of its signatories, the by now aged Father Longobardo, realized what he had been drawn into, and wrote again and personally to the vice-provincial urging that the trouble-makers should be removed from Peking if such could be arranged. There were others, too, whose responsibility it was to see things clearly and who did so. These were the three consultors to the vice-province, Father Brancato, Father Gravina and Father Smogulechi, whose advice to Dias would of course carry weight. All the same, though no direct action was taken (indeed apparently this would have been irregular if not impossible) the noise and smoke went on for some time. There are always those who take an excited interest in controversies of this kind, especially when personalities are involved, and de Magalhães had a real gift for fanning the flames. Father Schall was exonerated, as it were, more than once; finally by the

authorities in Rome with whom, of course, lay the ultimate responsibility for the Chinese mission.

Adam Schall himself did not join in the squabble on this point.
It is quite possible he was too proud to do so; also indifferent to
such things when he had his all-important work to get on with.
There is no doubt that some people were stung by his quick
retorts, his humorous but biting sarcasm and general unwillingness or inability to suffer fools very gladly. He at least knew
these faults, confessed them and deplored them.

His work, too, came under personal attack; but also and more
reasonably it was carefully examined by the authorities at home.
As a private astronomer and mathematician, from time to time
presenting the ministry of rites with the results of his studies
and observations, there was nothing to challenge. But a certain
wisdom in Schall's own extreme unwillingness to accept the
position of Director of the Institute of Astronomy becomes very
clear.

There was the fact of office itself, to start with. Adam Schall
had taken the solemn vows of poverty, chastity and obedience
and also five simple vows devised for the Society of Jesus by St
Ignatius, one of which was to refuse to accept any dignity or
official position. This has been the subject of considerable discussion and modification, so that today for example Jesuit
bishops may be found in some parts of the world. But at that
time it was certainly one of the more pertinent questions which
de Maghalhães raised, or rather, raised again, as when Schall
was first offered the position it was one of the obvious queries
to come under the consideration of his immediate superiors. The
general view seems to have been that St Ignatius had in mind
ecclesiastical position, with the purpose of keeping his priests
free and mobile in a way which they could not be for instance
as bishop of a diocese, and also of safeguarding them from becoming involved in the politics of ecclesiastical preferment, only
too apparent in the world he saw about him. The other argu-

ment, which suggested perhaps a little romantically that members of the Society must in their humility refuse all dignities of any kind was, as Schall himself remarked, difficult to maintain in view of the fact that Jesuits were already distinguished in academic positions, as rectors, or heads of colleges for example. It was in this light that, once having accepted it, he viewed his directorship of the Institute of Astronomy.

The question became one of considerable dimensions, involving good and honest men on either side; but more complex still was that of the actual duties of the Director and this gave rise to long and sometimes acrimonious discussion. As we have seen, the Institute of Astronomy came under the aegis of the ministry of rites; its function was to observe and record and, when required, forecast the movements of the heavenly bodies in order that the auspicious or inauspicious days and times might be known. These were all shown in the official Calendar. This, the Calendar of the Planets, was presented to the emperor and the minister of rites. But the Institute had also to produce another, popular, form of the Calendar, sometimes known from the colour of its covers as the Yellow Calendar. The first of these was an inoffensive work of astronomy; but the second was a great deal more dubious, containing as we have seen a large proportion of more or less superstitious popular beliefs. For instance, while setting out times of sunrise and sunset, the times when the sun entered the various sections of the zodiac, the phases of the moon and movements of the planets, it also stated what days were under the sway of good or evil spirits and informed its readers about the spirits which frequented houses or affected different parts of the human body.[1] Every day of the year was

[1] Cf. Shakespeare, *Twelfth Night*, Act i, Scene 3:
    Sir Toby: What shall we do else: were we not born under Taurus?
    Sir Andrew: Taurus? That's sides and heart.
    Sir Toby: No sir, it is legs and thighs: let me see thee caper!
    The relevance of this quotation from sixteenth-century Europe, especially in relation to the spirits and the heavens, becomes even more apparent below.

auspicious or inauspicious; on inauspicious days it was forbidden even to sweep the floor or to shave; it was perilous, even for the most weighty reasons, to dig a hole, enter into a legal agreement, marry, bury the dead or, perhaps surprisingly, offer sacrifice. At the end of the Yellow Calendar appeared the signature of the Director of the Institute of Astronomy and those of his assistants. Could a Jesuit Father, then, take the responsibility of directly overseeing the production of such a work, in which superstition played as large, or a larger, part than science?

The question was bound to arise sooner or later. For Adam Schall it was one of great moment. Having at last been pressed into the acceptance of the post, the Yellow Calendar became for him an integral part of his work. To give the position up again would be a profound blow, not least for its likely repercussions on the court and the people at large.

Some three years after Schall became Director, early in 1648, Father Giulio Aleni, then vice-provincial, had expressed his doubts about its suitability. But this was in no sense a personal criticism of Schall, nor a decision, and the prudent Italian had let the matter rest. It was, however, too promising a subject for the embittered Father Magalhães to ignore. In his eyes, Father Schall was violating not only the constitution of the Society but the requirements of plain morality. In 1649 he threw himself into the fray. With his talent for stirring up people's feelings he managed to gain support from other distinguished Jesuit Fathers including, of course, his companion, Father Buglio; among them was Father Furtado, who had instructed Schall to accept the post—Schall's private reactions may perhaps be imagined. (It is said that Furtado had developed some ill-will towards Schall.)

De Magalhães drew up a long document of some thirty-six pages to which he claimed the agreement of the other Fathers, though it is doubtful whether they even knew sufficient of the document to be in a position to approve it in detail. In it he sets out, in very proper order and argument of correct style, why a Jesuit should not fill the post of Director of the astronomical Institute. The first part is a consideration of the nature of superstition itself with an account of some decisions of the Church on the matter. The second applies these considerations to the Institute and the Calendar. In the third, becoming even more precise, he sets out ten reasons why Father Schall must, then, resign. The reasons include such statements as Schall's own danger of excommunication because of his close connection with superstitious practices, the risk to the good name of the Society, and indeed the Director's own danger of execution should he make some mistake in one of his official reports. The arguments all rest fundamentally on the question, which we have already met, of a Jesuit accepting official dignities and on the superstitious nature of the Director's work. Here again we may remind ourselves of the names of Father Gravina, Father Brancato and Father Smogulechi, Schall's firm supporters; Brancato in particular made sure that the authorities in Europe were kept informed of Schall's side of the controversy.

There were others too who needed no convincing of the honesty of Father Schall's position. But this was not a question which even Schall could brush away. He wrote a number of letters to the above-named Fathers, the consultors to the vice-provincial, and followed with a full letter of explanation to the general of the Society, dated March 7, 1652. In these he set himself to give an answer to three questions. Does the Institute of Astronomy in effect practise divination? Do the Calendar and the official reports contain superstitious elements? Is the Director of the Institute responsible for the aberrations to be found in the Calendar?

Schall returned a plain no, to the first. We do attribute to the stars, he says, a certain influence on human actions; we seek to expound celestial phenomena; we mention the names of spirits in the Calendar, but in all this we pay every regard to God. The first of these statements may sound surprising, but Schall was of his time. It is not always realized that the impetus behind the sixteenth and seventeenth centuries' profound desire to have more certain knowledge of the heavenly bodies was not so much a devotion to material scientific fact, as we understand it, as a rather sophisticated and perhaps fanciful philosophy of the relations between the heavens and the earth. Copernicus, Tycho Brahe, Galileo, still lived before the times when knowledge came to be shut up in subject boxes as it were, each with its separate key. They were inheritors of the Greeks and the Middle Ages, though with their own particular 'slant'; and it was the medieval Thomas Aquinas who wrote: 'The stars [governed by angels] influence the bodies of men and thus their temperaments, which are affected by their bodily constitution.[1] Normally a man will follow the bent of his character. In this sense therefore it may be said that human actions are immediately influenced by the stars. At the time of birth this influence is especially strong, which is why a largely accurate horoscope may then be cast of the course of this or that human life.'

Astrology as a whole was not then instinctively suspect as it is today. No wonder Schall evinced surprise at criticism which would involve also the use made of calendars in Christian Europe. Are we wrong, he asks, to see meteors and comets, all the moving world of the heavens, as signs of God's will? He cites learned men of irreproachable orthodoxy; and calls on the witness of Holy Scripture. The *Magi* [probably Persian astrologers] eagerly followed the leading of a star; the planet, the earth, shook in an earthquake at the death of Christ. Have we any reason to suppose that God no longer uses such means

---

[1] It is one of the greater ironies how men forget and have to relearn. Psychosomatic medicine has been hailed by some as deriving from a new understanding of the constitution of the human animal.

to teach men, and especially to make his voice heard by kings heedless of the cries of their subjects? As for making use of the names of various spirits, they merely signify stars. Are we disturbed in mind when we refer similarly to Venus, Jupiter, Mars, or Saturn?

He goes on to say that when Christians in the astronomical Institute place the word 'sacrifice' by certain dates, their personal intention is to enjoin on men the virtues of heedfulness and humility especially fitting in those who offer sacrifice. In its relation to the idolatrous acts of immolation in honour of gods or spirits, it is an indication not a command. He compares the calendar of the Benedictine, Father Buccellini, which notes the days on which the ancient Romans offered their sacrifices; or the practice of Catholic rulers who publish the days of devotion observed by the Jews or Protestants among their subjects. He concludes firmly: 'No, the Institute of Astronomy does not practise divination; nor does it have any dealings with occult, diabolic or other suspect forces.'

Father Schall answers the second of his questions by emphasizing the nature of the Calendar and his work on it: 'All that we are doing is to repeat yet again the traditions of centuries. We make no kind of guarantee of value or truth.' To the final question of the Director's responsibility for what goes into the Calendar, he declares that he can have none. It is not his place (whether Buddhist or Christian) to meddle with what is already laid down and has been laid down from time immemorial, even though recognizing himself its varied and often dubious character. In this sense, the Director is the servant of the Calendar. The part played by Adam Schall is made plain to all by the public decree which stated that his task was to oversee the astronomical observations 'according to the new scientific methods of the Europeans'.

Schall concludes by asking with some anxiety whether this is sufficiently clear and well put. With something of the air of a peasant watching a hail-storm spread towards his precious harvest, he makes a concluding appeal: 'We realize most fully that all is not yet complete or faultless. Our great desire and aim is to give the Chinese Calendar a Christian character as soon as possible. However, even as it is, the work is not to be despised. It maintains the Fathers in Peking, and supports them in their missionary labours. But if our work should be so unfortunate as to be condemned it would mean the unleashing afresh of hatred or contempt among those who have begun to be our friends because they have learned to value us; it could bring the speedy expulsion of Christian leaders from China and the end of the mission.'

It was now in the hands of the appropriate authorities whose decision, it would appear from the foregoing, must rest on principles of moral theology concerning the nature of responsibility. The general, Father Nickel, called a commission of five theologians of the Roman College who, in 1655, made a number of interim observations not entirely favourable to Father Schall. They were unanimous that nothing could be objected to in that part of the Calendar for which Schall was directly responsible. They did not consider that Schall's official post need necessarily be condemned, but at the same time they emphasized the question of the superstitious elements in the Calendar, making it clear that there were circumstances in which Schall should resign. But did these circumstances now obtain? As is clear from these rather ambiguous statements, they were not confident that they were in full command of the facts of the case, and the discussions continued.

In the meantime, Schall quite correctly remained where he was; and weighty support grew. Twice in 1660 Father Simon da Cunha, visitor apostolic to the vice-province, wrote vigorously in his favour. In 1661, Father Ferdinand Verbiest produced a kind of detailed apologia for the work of the man he respected so greatly. One of the points he made was in relation to the spirits which were causing so much trouble. He declares that the Chinese of early times (when the Calendar was first formed) did not believe superstitiously in spirits, and therefore they were not really intended in this sense in the Calendar. He also points out that the Chinese are almost slavish traditionalists. That the Calendar itself is largely a convention is shown by the fact that after each cycle of sixty years the official drawing it up makes an exact repetition of what has been set out before. This has a direct bearing on accusations of superstitious beliefs about the influence of the stars on men; the importance of the contents of the Calendar for the Chinese people lies in their profound respect for the customs and rites of antiquity. This whole work of Verbiest's made a great impression, evoking for instance the plaint that if only such an exhaustive exposition had been available before much or all of the controversy could have been avoided.

This speech for the defence (a role in which Father Verbiest was soon to prove himself invaluable) was not even known in Rome when, early in 1664, a new commission came to a decision fully in Adam Schall's favour—we have always to remember the time-lag caused by the long and perilous journey. Four theologians of the Roman College addressed their conclusions to the father general and the vicar general, Father John Paul Oliva. They declared plainly that: 'The Director of the Institute is in no way responsible for anything superstitious which the Calendar as such may contain.' As for holding the post itself: 'Father Schall might exercise the functions and wear the insignia of imperial mathematician with complete confidence. For final confirmation, however, it is right that this should be referred to the Holy See;' this latter no doubt was in recognition of the fact that it is the Holy See which ultimately authorizes the constitution and rule of a religious order, and also perhaps of the Society's especial and unusually direct orientation towards the pope. In April of the same year, Pope Alexander VII pro-

nounced: 'In view of the manifest advantages for the propagation of the faith afforded by the post of official astronomer, the
Holy Father grants all dispensations that may be required in
order that members of the Society may accept it.' This made
the way plain, without entanglement in what might or might not
have been the intentions of St Ignatius; the rule is not an im-
mutable moral law. The concern of the general had been increased by Father da Cunha's urgent request from China for a
definite decision. Father Oliva was now able to write to de Cunha
for him, not only giving the favourable reply but asking him
to encourage Father Schall and, if possible, to prepare someone suitable to take in due course the now ageing Schall's place.

Thus the answer came; the work and methods of Father
John Adam Schall were approved and safeguarded. There was
general satisfaction; the majority of those who had opposed
Schall had done so on real questions of certain principles and
their interpretation, and were glad without personal 'feeling'
to have these elucidated by the authorities at home. Only the
indefatigable Father de Magalhães remained unconvinced. Sur-
viving Schall, he continued the struggle to the end of his life,
addressing himself to Father Verbiest who, as Schall's successor, took his place in the mind of the unhappy man as the
great example of a proud and unworthy Jesuit.

Adam Schall himself most probably never received the decision. He died before the letter crossed the seas and continents.
His last few years were passed with this great question always
at the back of his mind; nor did he have more immediate consolations. These were years of suffering.

The Way of the Cross

THE outlook at the death of the emperor Shun-chih was not set fair. Even before the young man's death Adam Schall was becoming that inviting target for the attacks of the jealous and the ambitious, the great councillor who was falling from favour. Now again the emperor was a child, and there was a regency once more. As we have seen in the official recognition of the boy Schall had adopted, there was no immediate or universal revival of hostility. But the clouds were gathering.

The leader of the attack was Yang Kuang-hsien, an old man of seventy but one who still possessed all the qualities of ambition and cruelty, vigour and real intelligence which had marked his adventurous career. Under the last of the Ming emperors he had been banished to Liaotung; but the Manchus had allowed his return and he had found a post in one of the ministries of state. His hostility towards Adam Schall was personal in so far as the Director of the Institute of Astronomy was a great man in high position, and moreover it appears that Yang had some pretensions to science himself. But his real aim was first to bring down Schall, and in his train all Chinese Christianity.

The first revealing skirmish came when, in 1659 or 1660, he published a 'Refutation of the Noxious Doctrine'. This contained three parts, and in them he made the following charges: 'Christianity perverts the Chinese way of life: it forbids people to pay proper and fitting respect to the emperor and the family, and criticises the reverence due to our ancestors. It makes a discord in the universal harmony and thus damages the well-being of the State. The missionaries are really conspirators in the pay of Portugal.' These accusations are familiar enough, and no doubt Yang was not interested in originality. What was fresh was the force, even violence, of expression. Nevertheless, it did not appear especially dangerous, and was for a long time left unanswered.

This attack, and others like it, might have slipped into oblivion but for two things: after a time the ever-ready Father de Magalhães and Father Buglio took up the challenge, and Yang himself found a really dangerous charge which he made against the Christians. The reply of the two Jesuits appeared in 1664 under the title, 'The Origin and Propagation of the Divine Law'. It contained these imposing lines: 'Christianity is the most ancient and most perfect of all religions. It is to be found inscribed in the hearts of all men. It was proclaimed to the first human beings, and engraved by God himself on two stone tablets. Ancient books bear witness that Christianity was the early religion of China; the apostle St Thomas sent one of his disciples to convert the Chinese, and other missionaries came through the ages to continue and extend this first apostolate; the [Nestorian] monument at Sianfu is certain proof of this. Finally, Father Matthew Ricci came to China and opened the way for his followers.' This historical résumé was concluded by some information on imperial genealogy: the first emperor was descended from Adam and came to China from the land of the Jews. As if to complete their work of controversy as tactlessly as possible, they then affirm that: 'Chinese learning and wisdom is only a pale reflection of Christian doctrine.' If it is bad argument to make statements which stand in need of proof, it is still less excusable to offer up one's adversaries on the altar of one's own thesis. The statements made by the two enthusiasts were often clumsy, unjust and wounding; nothing was more calculated to antagonize the Chinese than the suggestion that their revered age-old civilization had been derived from the West. The two Fathers had presented the enemies of Christianity with a sheaf of arrows.

Yang Kuang-hsien answered with, 'I can not keep silent'. In this, the most offensive of the Jesuits' statements were pinpointed, and his previous charges amplified and increased by remarks of the following kind: 'The eclipse of the sun which they say took place at the death of Christ is pure invention: it was not observed in China. Christ himself was only a revolutionary, rightly executed. The missionaries are simply undesirable agitators who were driven out of Europe and have now come to China to preach rebellion to the people. They wish to gain control of China, using Macao as their base.' Father Buglio returned to the attack with his, 'I reply because I also can not keep silent'.

All this was in the main advantageous only to Yang. Father Schall, in the footsteps of Matthew Ricci, had repeatedly warned and advised his colleagues against any denigration of the great teachers of China and the ancient institutions of the empire. But here were two Fathers who seemed to be going out of their way to demonstrate publicly that it was the anti-Christian Yang who was the real champion of Chinese civilization. Yang also had more direct and powerful supporters in the persons of Oboi, one of the four Manchu regents, and En Ko-te, former minister of rites, now returned from banishment and still nursing his resentment against Schall.

On April 20 of the same year, 1664, Adam Schall had a stroke. He was considerably paralysed, barely able to speak or write and hardly able to walk. On September 15, Yang Kuang-hsien returned to the attack. He presented a petition to the Board of Rites charging Schall and his companions with treachery, preaching an abominable religion and teaching false astronomical methods. It was in the last accusation that his master-stroke (and the influence of En Ko-te) appeared, for he revived as an example the tragically inauspicious time of the burial of the late Shun-chih's little son with the 'resultant' deaths of both the boy's mother and then the emperor himself. Though the fault as we know had been that of the minister of rites, it was easy to place it on the shoulders of the Director of the Institute of Astronomy; and this was serious, for it struck at the heart of confidence in Father Schall.

He was arrested, and with him Ferdinand Verbiest and, per-haps a little ironically, Buglio and de Magalhães (who had been virtually free for a number of years); also a number of Chinese Christians associated with the astronomical Institute. They were brought before a court which sat in the hall of the ministry of rites. Schall's condition was pathetic, and an official brought him a mat to sit on.

The main indictments, to which the prisoners were required to give an immediate preliminary answer, were read out, and Schall, who was the principal target, replied through the mouth of Father Verbiest. First of all: 'Schall only took charge of the Institute of Astronomy in order to build churches more easily and to propagate Christianity in China.' The answer to this was that the emperor himself had imposed these scientific duties on him; this imperial command is engraved on the column set up outside the church, plainly, for all to read. Then: 'These ignorant foreigners declare that the first emperor of China came from Europe.' What were Schall's thoughts at this moment? But he could no longer indulge in one of his ironic and humorous exclamations; he answered through Verbiest with some diplomacy that: 'It is our opinion that he was a native of

Palestine, but this is in fact situated in a part of Asia.' The third charge concerned the *Agnus Dei* and such like blessed objects of piety which it was the custom of the Jesuit Fathers to give to their catechumens and which were now stated to be used in the practice of sorcery. Finally, each of the prisoners was required to say what part he had played in the composition and publication of 'The Origin and Propagation of the Divine Law'.

The accused were now permitted to return home, and Adam Schall had himself conveyed by the way of his church where he prayed in his enforced silence while his flock lifted up their voices and wept in distress around him. But this was only the beginning. The inquiry continued, its formal object being to establish the relative guilt of each of the accused, but resolving itself more and more clearly into three questions: Is Adam Schall a traitor to the State? Has he propagated an obnoxious religion? Has he taught a false system of astronomy?

Schall's treachery is obvious, maintained Yang Kuang-hsien. We have only to open our eyes to see signs of it everywhere. Baptism is given only to the privately initiated; confession is a stratagem by which passwords and details of the coming attack may be given in secret; there are twenty thousand men stationed at Macao, only waiting the word to back up these agitators by force of arms. Thus he reviewed all the Fathers' activities, interpreting them with great ingenuity as the actions of conspirators. This went on for twelve days. However, the court failed to be outraged by Yang's sensational revelations, even with the aid of a shower of gold pieces. The case was really too clear. Everyone knew that it was the emperor himself who had given the Jesuit Fathers official permission to enter China; the bureaucratic Chinese civil service had all the documents filed for reference. As for little Macao, it was difficult to take it seriously as a military threat to the empire. It was equally hard to see the European missionaries, who were still few in number and scattered over a vast area, as being in a position to concoct plots. Any Chinese could not but answer such accusations as easily as the Fathers themselves.

Among the charges in relation to the 'obnoxious religion' which Schall was accused of preaching were that it had caused him to renounce his native land and to live a celibate. These were rather cleverly chosen to appeal to Chinese ways of thought. Father Verbiest made an excellent defence lawyer; he drew the attention of the court to the fact that Confucius himself, at least for a time, had done the same. The third question, that of astronomical methods was left aside for the time being.

All in all, Yang Kuang-hsien was hardly delighted with the results of the inquiry. He gave the accused three weeks respite and used the time to win support by the distribution of many thousands of *taels* and to stir up public opinion. On November 12 he had his first real victory: the four Fathers were committed to prison, being held in chains as was the Chinese custom, though the conditions were at first alleviated for the Director of the Institute of Astronomy. Thus they were to live for six months. The inquiries and examinations continued. On December 27, the minister of rites made a long list of charges: Adam Schall had the insolence to teach that Christ, an executed criminal, is the Lord of heaven and earth; he has been baptizing two or three hundred Chinese every year; to the new Christians he has given objects relating to his religion and a calendar of its festivals; it is he who was responsible for the [never to be forgotten] 'Origin and Propagation of the Divine Law'; he claims deceitfully that the late emperor Shun-chih in condemning false sects did not include Christianity; he teaches that all men are descended from Adam and that all must honour the God of Christians; the words 'according to the new method' placed in certain parts of the Calendar are an insult to China; he leads the people astray with his talk of the wondrous effects of baptism, confession and the last rites; he teaches that the heavens

are simply God's throne and not God himself; he forbids the
worship paid to ancestors by sacrifice and offerings; he has
suspicious dealings with Macao and, after having first admitted
it, he then denied it, and that proves him a liar; four times in
each month he gathers the Christians together and collects
money [an unusual view of Sunday Mass!].

The consequences of this fine tirade were all that Yang could
have desired. Schall was stripped of title, rank and dignities, and
henceforward, sick man as he was, he lived in chains with his
companions. All the Christian places of worship, except the
church which Schall had built with imperial support, were to be
destroyed; other missionaries were to be called to Peking, while
the prisoners were handed over to the minister of justice for
sentence. This was passed on January 15, 1665: 'Unless the
supreme court of justice reduces the sentence, Adam Schall,
the chief of the traitors, is to be put to death by strangulation;
Fathers Verbiest, Buglio and de Magalhães, and Li Tsu-pe
[with other Christian officials of the Institute of Astronomy]
are to receive one hundred strokes of the cane and then to be
exiled.'

There was still the third accusation to be considered: Has
Adam Schall taught a false system of astronomy? While the
supreme court deliberated, the minister of justice turned his
attention to this (whether in over-confidence or with some idea
that justice should be seen to be done, is not clear). This was,
in any case, easily put to the test, with the heavens themselves
as witness. An eclipse of the sun was expected, and Chinese,
Muslim and Christian astronomers all differed as to the exact
time at which it would take place. The Chinese stated a quarter
past two in the afternoon, the Muslims half past two, and Father
Verbiest in his prison with Schall had calculated three o'clock.
There was a great gathering of astronomers and other officials
in the astronomical institute. A quarter past two came and
nothing happened, half past two and still nothing. At three, a

public crier announced that this was the hour declared by T'ang Jo-wang, and hardly had he spoken when the first shadow was seen on the sun's face. As a matter of fact Father Verbiest, who was hardly well situated at the time for mathematics, realized afterwards that he had miscalculated by a few minutes; but in the excitement of the moment no one noticed it. He had also predicted that it would be a nearly total eclipse, and this was so. This triumph of the European astronomers received considerable publicity, being reported in the Imperial Gazette.

The supreme court, however, remained unmoved. On February 4 its three judges ratified the sentence of the minister of justice. It now required the signatures of the regents but, in spite of Oboi's influence, they hesitated. Schall was if anything now more than ever a famous man; they dared not forget how the late emperor Shun-chih had praised Schall's religion, and Shun-chih's mother, still alive, spoke forcibly in criticism of those who were attacking her son's friend. In bringing down Schall, they did not want to imperil their own position and power, and this placed the conspirators in a quandary. Schall's answers to the other accusations had been sufficiently convincing to dispel any hopes the regents had of making headway by repeating them, and they were thrown back again on the rather desperate hope of even yet discrediting the Europeans' astronomy.

There then took place a series of examinations before the Grand Council of the Crown itself, Adam Schall again answering through Ferdinand Verbiest, both bearing the weight of their chains. This had the advantage of removing the responsibility from the regents and placing it on the shoulders of a large number of Manchu princes and officials many of whom were hostile to the accused and most, if not all, ignorant of science. Schall himself was often so exhausted that he lay on the floor while the 'judges' looked on pitilessly. After ten sittings the judgment came, unanimous but for the voices of two ministers who refused to have anything to do with it. The regents, led by Oboi, signed the decree.

Once again John Adam Schall was condemned to death, this time by beheading, a fate which his Chinese companions from the Institute of Astronomy were to share. The penalty for the other three Jesuits remained unchanged. But this was not yet severe enough for regent Oboi. He changed the form of the death sentence: Schall was to suffer the *ling-ch'ih,* the most barbarous of all deaths known to Chinese law, by which the victim was literally but slowly cut to pieces with a sharp sword while each wound was cauterized with a red hot iron to prevent too quick a death through loss of blood.

Father Schall faced this. What his inmost thoughts were we cannot know, though all his life would bear witness to a willingness, eagerness, to live and die for and like his Master. His sufferings up to that time had not been slight: the paralysed body, in heavy chains day and night, dragging itself to examination after examination; worst of all for a man like Schall, the paralysed speech: no longer able to stand up and face his accusers with quick mind and ready tongue. He knew to the full that helplessness which is not the least of the pains of martyrdom: 'As a young man, thou wouldst gird thyself and walk where thou hadst the will to go, but when thou has grown old, thou wilt stretch out thy hands, and another shall gird thee, and carry thee where thou goest, not of thy own will' (St John's Gospel, chapter 21). Perhaps, with a flash of his old robust humour, he wondered how long a body which had already gone through so much would survive...

Then the heavens came to the aid of the man who had plotted their courses with such loving care. On April 13 a comet appeared in the sky. The planet, the earth, also played its part. The formality of the boy emperor's signature was required on the death warrant and at the moment the warrant was being conveyed to him for this purpose, at eleven o'clock in the morn-

ing on April 16, an earthquake struck Peking. The imperial
palace shook so that the emperor ran outside in affright;
the city walls were breached in many places and houses collapsed. Schall himself saw one of the prison walls come down,
while gaolers fled to join the terrified crowds in the streets where
cracks gaped at their feet. The cross over Schall's church
crashed to the ground. The tremors took two days to subside,
while the wind blew about the clouds of dust which rose in the
air and obscured the sun.

Friends of the Christians were heartened in their vocal support of the prisoners, enemies were alarmed; both felt that
heaven and earth were speaking. The scared authorities at once
took certain steps; on April 19, an amnesty was granted which
included Ferdinand Verbiest, Buglio, de Magalhães and one of
the Chinese Christian officials. Four days later, the death
sentence on Adam Schall was commuted; but he remained in
chains, until, so it seemed, nature took a hand again. On April
29 fire raged in the imperial palace; some forty rooms were
burnt out and there were people who claimed that they had seen
a fire-ball descend on the building. All Peking was now terrified;
the God of the Christians is himself upholding the cause of his
servants, was the cry, and the voices could not be calmed.

The authorities had gone as far as they had dared, and in a
few cases as far as they wished. While five of the Christians
from the astronomical institute were beheaded, churches closed
(not destroyed) and, later, thirty missionaries who had been
called to Peking banished together to Canton, Father Schall was
at last set free. On May 23, two days before Pentecost, the
official seals that had been placed on the Jesuit residence were
removed, and Father Schall returned to his home.

Yang Kuang-hsien continued to vent his spite, though without much effect. On Whit Monday he led a gang of hired ruffians to ransack Schall's church; early in June he broke up the
inscribed column which had been set up in Schall's honour out-

side the church—and sent him the pieces. Eight times he published attacks on the European astronomer, and thrice were Schall and Verbiest constrained to appear before the minister of rites. Adam Schall knew no real repose again on earth.

Yet, as if he considered that he had not been humbled enough, as if still conscious of those faults and failings of temperament which we have not overlooked, Father Schall prepared himself for death by dictating to the ever devoted Ferdinand Verbiest a public confession to which his hand, partially paralysed and till so recently in chains, was just able to write an almost unrecognizable signature. This confession, which is also by way of being his testament, Ferdinand Verbiest read to other of the Jesuit fathers gathered around the sick man's bed.

Reverend Fathers in Christ: I would have liked today to place myself before you in that position in which but lately I appeared before the heathen judges for the sake of the Catholic religion. With chains round my neck, bent head, fettered like a criminal, a humble suppliant, so would I have stretched out my hands to you, thus showing forth my sincere repentance and grief of soul. Alas, my sickness makes such a gesture impossible. I present myself, therefore, as I am before this Community which represents for me the whole Society of Jesus. I am not going to defend myself as I did a few months ago in the courts, but rather to charge myself in full honesty and candour. To you all and to each of you individually I confess that during the years past I have given bad example and caused scandal [in the theological sense]. I have sinned above all in relation to my superiors: I have not always observed their counsel or advice and, more seriously still, I have found fault with them in both what I have said and what I have written. I charge myself especially with having been disproportionately indulgent towards my servant so that he has been a source of offence to many but in particular to my colleagues in this house; his rudeness and impudence must largely be laid to my account. Contrary to the vow of poverty, I have often gone to unnecessary expenditure.

In adopting my servant's son I was guilty of imprudence. I
have caused scandal, and offended against brotherly love by
word and by pen, especially among my colleagues in this city;
and in seeking to satisfy the demands of my assistants I have
deprived my brothers of many requirements.

In all these and many other things, I acknowledge myself
guilty. With a contrite heart, I strike my breast and scatter ashes
on my bent head, repeating ever and again (in so far as I can
speak at all): 'Through my fault, through my fault, through my
most grievous fault.' I beg you reverend Fathers who see me here
paralysed, nailed to my bed, to believe that, as formerly before
the judges of the courts, now equally chained I kneel before
religious authority, guilty as I am but with a contrite heart awaiting judgment.

Lastly, I beg that no one takes this confession as an after-
thought or as having been extorted by adversity; it was not indeed the fruit of my own thought but of the will of the merciful
God who touches the hearts of men with gentleness and power
at the times and in the manner which his providence and grace
ordain. The moment chosen for me has been when God, the loving and merciful Father, has laid his hand on both body and
soul. Since the compassionate God has in his patience enabled
me to live even till now in the Society of his Son, so I have full
trust that, on account of your prayers and blessed works, he
will grant me perseverance to the end and keep me with his
grace. Amen.—Peking, July 21, 1665. John Adam Schall.

When Father Schall dictated this confession, which must
have moved his secretary taking it down even more than it does
us three centuries later, he supposed that death was very close.
In fact he lived another year. It was not a year of great promise.
Four Jesuit Fathers were permitted to remain in Peking but they
were not allowed to teach their 'execrable doctrine' and an
official was instructed to keep surveillance over them. Still more
discouraging to Schall himself, the regent Oboi appointed Yang
Kuang-hsien, who really knew very little about the matter, head

of the Institute of Astronomy. He took Schall's place in the imperial astronomer's official residence and for three years carried on there as well as he could. Schall saw his work taken out of his hands and apparently falling to pieces under the incompetent control of an enemy who pursued him with his hatred quite literally to the day of his death.

We remember too that he still did not know the decision of the Jesuit authorities at home and the Holy See on his whole work as imperial astronomer; he could wonder on his deathbed whether the great achievement of his life was for nothing. It was a desolation known to the saints; a reflection of the desolation of their Master on the cross. Adam Schall had his faithful companion and disciple also; Ferdinand Verbiest was his interpreter and spokesman and indeed his nurse, and was to be, though at the time neither knew it, his successor.

The sick man was failing visibly. His breathing grew increasingly heavy and difficult, and there were times when he lost consciousness. Until August 8, 1666, he had managed to sit out of bed for an hour or two a day, but this was no longer possible; and he was given the Last Sacraments. Like the light in an oil lamp when its fuel runs low, the flame of his life wavered and flickered and sank. At last, at four o'clock in the afternoon on August 15, the feast of the Assumption or the *Dormitio*—the 'Falling Asleep'—of our blessed Lady, John Adam Schall died, his brethren and servants around him. On August 29, the commemoration of the martyrdom of St John the Baptist, five hundred Christians escorted his body to its resting-place near that of Matthew Ricci in what was to become the famous Catholic Christian cemetery of Peking.

Ferdinand Verbiest, who wrote a description of Father Schall's last days, speaks thus of the man whom he loved and respected so greatly: 'After forty years of work in the Lord's vineyard, this faithful servant—thus did providence permit—was stripped of everything which gives satisfaction to human life and became the victim of intense suffering. This great apostle, who himself could not speak of the passion of our Saviour without tears, was found worthy to be shaped, through the instrumentality of his enemies, into a likeness of our crucified Lord.' Father Verbiest concludes: 'These are my words concerning him whom I loved as a father. It is not a panegyric, but a simple account of his life. . . .'

Epilogue

THERE is a good deal to be said against the custom of some biographers who end their task abruptly with their subject's death, giving no word to the fortunes of their posthumous fame or the times and circumstances in which they may have played a striking part. Yet, if it be a temptation, it is perhaps not surprising if it is sometimes yielded to. To give a wholly adequate account of 'what happened afterwards' would commonly require another book. But here certainly a brief sketch, or at least a few indications, must be attempted. The history of Christianity in China yesterday and today is not so unimportant, or so well known, that we can treat the life of John Adam Schall as that of an interesting man who lived in stirring times, but of no wider relevance or significance.

At the time of his death, Father Schall may have needed all his not slight faith and hope when he considered the state of the Christian mission; and yet this time was a turning-point. The key figure was still really Adam Schall himself. Almost at once after his death his colleagues were confirmed and encouraged by the arrival of the letter of formal approbation from Rome. In 1668, the young emperor K'ang-hsi (who, we may remember, as Shun-chih's son owed his imperial throne largely to Schall) took the reins of government into his own hands. He immediately showed himself both percipient and determined. A copy of the Calendar which the old enemy Yang Kuang-hsien had produced when he took Schall's place at the Institute of Astronomy was sent for Father Verbiest's opinion. His report on it was so bad that the emperor ordered a commission to be set up, and the result was that in 1669 Yang was relieved of his post and later in the same year Ferdinand Verbiest was appointed Director of the Institute.

K'ang-hsi turned his attention also to his former regent, Oboi, who had numerous other crimes against his name as well as his attack on the late Director of the astronomical institute; he died in prison. An inquiry was directed into the proceedings against Adam Schall and his colleagues, of which the immediate result was the final disgrace of Yang Kuang-hsien, who died as he was going into exile from the capital. This was followed by the rehabilitation of the Christian mission in China, and in the first place of Father Schall himself. His titles and ranks were posthumously restored (a transaction which held no irony in Chinese official eyes) as were the ranks of those Christian members of the Institute of Astronomy who had been executed; while property which had been confiscated was restored to the Jesuit Fathers. The Grand Council of the Crown and the emperor agreed: 'It is our firm belief that the Christian religion contains nothing that can be censured; it may be publicly professed;' and the title, 'Eminent Master of the Celestial Law' was conferred on the late T'ang Jo-wang. For a short while the banished missionary priests remained herded together at Canton while the emperor gave his government a breathing-space; then in 1671 they were allowed to return to their various posts throughout the empire, and churches and houses were restored to them.

The reign of K'ang-hsi was perhaps the greatest period for Catholic Christianity in China. His great 'Edict of Toleration' of March 22, 1692 was itself prompted by the president of the Board of Rites among others, and expressed a new empire-wide official view of Christianity. At the same time the mission was able to build on the work and ideas of such men as Ricci, Schall and Verbiest; that is to say, not only did Christianity spread rapidly but the building up of the Church in China seemed to be based on viable principles with a clear purpose and method.

Subsequent developments are perhaps of more detailed interest to the historian than the general reader, not only in their extreme complexity, but because our view of China today has been overshadowed by a new revolution, another abrupt change of government, perhaps (in spite of its theoretical basis) even leading to the founding of a new dynasty in the Chinese fashion: who can tell? In the meantime the fortunes of the Church had been variable. Emperors and authorities were by no means always favourable; while the activities of Western Powers, more political or nationalistic than concerned with spiritual principles, too often proved disastrous. The Church was to know many more martyrs, the most celebrated being those of the Boxer 'rebellion' in the year 1900. Nor had all been well within. This is no place to go into the details, let alone the rights and wrongs, of the notorious Rites controversy. In general terms, the Jesuit attempt to assimilate in every possible way to Chinese modes of life and thought, including even the toleration of certain 'religious' rites, came under heavy fire from their fellows in other religious orders and exercised the minds of a series of popes. The principle at stake is perhaps not difficult; but its application—is this, in these circumstances, superstition?—was very much so. There was no lack of discussion at all levels, but in due course formal prohibition came, most notably in the Bull of Benedict XIV, *Ex quo singulari*, in 1742. Its importance was this: in forbidding Christians to take part in the traditional rites or ceremonies (called Confucian, though in fact dating from before his time), it made the existence of Christian mandarins, as Adam Schall, or Paul Hsü Kuang-ch'i, had been, impossible. This was a loss to Chinese Christian life which it is hard to measure; and with it of course went the general result that Christianity was given the appearance of a religion for foreigners or for those who were anxious for some reason to cut themselves off from their neighbours. Remembering the approval formerly given to Adam Schall's work and his official post, and our present re-thinking of missionary activity in relation to fundamental Catholic principles and the practice of much earlier times which derives directly from the Holy See itself, we may well feel regret. But we need not pretend that it was an easy decision to come to, nor forget that any authority cannot but act on the evidence provided and it appears that, here, the Jesuits themselves were rather slow in making their case understood.

Nevertheless, the Church in China has been vital and vigorous. If the question of a vernacular liturgy, which would have gone far to solve many related problems, went by default (though of course the subject in relation to the world-wide Church is now under review), the first Chinese priest, the Jesuit Chêng Wei-hsin, was ordained in Rome as early as 1664 (that is, two years before Schall's death). Perhaps the most striking feature of the nineteenth century was the arrival of an extraordinary number and variety of religious orders from all parts the world, active and contemplative, priests, teachers, doctors and nurses; with this went the gradual foundation of a number of native religious congregations and, very important, in the twentieth century the consecration of Chinese bishops, first of all under the inspiration of Pope Pius XI acting on principles enunciated by his immediate predecessors.[1]

[1] It is also of interest to note that the first Protestant mission entered China in 1807 with the arrival of the Scot, Robert Morrison, sent by the London Missionary Society; he was followed by men and women of many nations, Swedes, Dutch, Germans, Americans. A number of Protestants witnessed with their lives to their faith in Christ, along with Catholics, in the Boxer outbreaks and massacres.

By 1907 there were a million Catholic Christians in China, by the time of the recent revolution something like two and a half million; an organized Christian body, with its dioceses and parishes, religious houses and seminaries, hospitals and education—elementary and higher. It is impossible to obtain an overall picture of what is now left; we can only obtain piecemeal information of destruction and persecution from the personal experience of those Christians (notably clergy) who have been sent across the border to Hong Kong rather than being imprisoned for life or put to death. One thing is certain: these Chinese lay people, men, women and children, these Chinese priests and bishops, who are resisting the demands of the new powers with such heroism are in the tradition of Matthew Ricci, Adam Schall and Ferdinand Verbiest, not only in their bearing under intense suffering but in their understanding of the Christian life, not least in its relationship with the state.[1] At the same time, the West is showing a new and lively interest in the character, ideas and work of such men; while preliminary steps in the cause for the beatification of Paul Hsü Kuang-chi and his grand-daughter Candida are being discussed.

Ferdinand Verbiest said of John Adam Schall that, along with his swift and lucid mind, rare gift for languages and remarkable

---

[1] In June, 1951, Father John Tung Chi-shih was put up by the new powers in Chungking to speak at a public demonstration intended to arouse enthusiasm for an 'autonomous Catholic Church', one which in effect severed its bond with the Holy See. His profoundly wise and just speech was not at all what the authorities had hoped for; he was arrested four weeks afterwards, as he was vesting for Mass, and only rumours have reached us as to his fate. Three of the things he said were:

Suppose that, moved by fear, I should act against my conscience, speak against my thoughts, and sign what I do not approve. Then I am openly deceiving the authorities. And if in private I admit that I said what I did not mean because I was forced, then I have been deceiving the bishops of the Church. That, surely, is the way to sow discord between the government and the Church.

I am a Catholic. But that does not prevent me from greatly admiring the communists for more than one quality.

memory, he accomplished so much through his profound and
devoted spiritual life, in which no public or private religious
duties were neglected, together with his realistic and genuine
approach to his scientific and astronomical studies—he was not
playing at them nor using them simply as a pawn. Most portraits of Father Schall, of which we have a number of varying
authenticity, show him as an old man with a long, thick beard
and a much lined and worn, almost mask-like, face; but in this
face his eyes shine out, alive, direct (and sometimes even with a
touch of mischief). They may remind us of the underlying fac-
tor in his life and character, the living faith, and deriving from
that faith in the ordinances and providence of God the un-
shakeable conviction that, in whatever vicissitudes, he was dedicated to a work which was not to die.

We have been fortunate in the recent publication of two detailed and lively accounts of the first Jesuits in China. Vincent
Cronin's *The Wise Man from the West* (Rupert Hart-Davis,
1955 and Fontana Books, 1961) presents a picture of the life
and work of Matthew Ricci. *Generation of Giants* by George
Dunne, S.J. (Burns & Oates, 1962) is an authoritative study
from the beginnings of the Mission in China to the death of
Adam Schall.

A more extended account of Father Tung and the substance
of his speech in June 1951 is given in: Donald Attwater:
Martyrs, from St Stephen to John Tung (Sheed and Ward,

I am a Chinese and I am a Catholic. I love my country and I love my
Church. I categorically reject all that is contrary to the laws of that
country and to the laws of that Church. Above all, I will not take part in
anything that might give rise to discord. But if Church and government
cannot reach agreement, then sooner or later no Chinese Catholic will have
any alternative but to die. Why, then, should I not offer up my life here
and now to hasten the mutual understanding of the two parties?
His conclusion is in terms at once very Chinese and very Catholic:
Please forgive all the shortcomings of this poor speech.
In the name of the Father and of the Son and of the Holy Ghost.
Amen.

1958). Another modern book (referred to at the beginning of this volume) which illuminates the greatness and timelessness of the Chinese Christian mind, reminding us at once of Ricci or Hsü Kuang-ch'i and the great thinkers of the early Church, is: Dom Pierre-Célestin Lou Tseng-Tsiang: *Ways of Confucius and of Christ* (Burns Oates, 1948).